THE REVELATION OF JOHN

An Exposition

THE REVELATION OF JOHN

An Exposition

by
CHARLES R. ERDMAN

PREFACE BY EARL F. ZEIGLER

THE WESTMINSTER PRESS

PHILADELPHIA

Published by The Westminster Press®
Philadelphia, Pennsylvania
PRINTED IN THE UNITED STATES OF AMERICA

To
My Children

PREFACE

The closing book of the New Testament contains about twelve thousand words. Concerning these "words" the writer of The Revelation says, "Blessed is he who reads aloud the words of the prophecy, and blessed are those who hear, and who keep what is written therein; for the time is near" (ch. 1:3). In the last chapter the writer issues a stern warning against any one adding to or taking away from "the words of the prophecy of this book."

Throughout the centuries the words of the book have remained intact, but millions have been the words that have been written to interpret this book. Commentaries in print, and out of print, are numerous. Many more will follow in their train. Some interpreters take the position that The Revelation is predictive prophecy with much of it still to be fulfilled. Others teach that it is predictive prophecy largely or completely fulfilled. But other interpreters accent the *pastoral* objective of the book—to encourage the early Christians to endure their violent persecutions (perhaps in the reign of the Emperor Domitian) with courageous abandon. They were assured that the Lamb (the glorified Christ) would conquer all his and their foes, and that a new heaven and a new earth would be the home of the redeemed.

With such "variant views" (and others not described), Dr. Charles R. Erdman was familiar when he was commissioned to write an exposition of this "most perplexing" book, to use his own words. He states that he approached his task with "diffidence," but with a conviction and confidence in "the practical and imperishable values of this portion of Scripture." Previously he had written sixteen volumes in the Erdman series of New Testament commentaries, and The Revelation would complete the entire New Testament. Time has proven that Dr. Erdman was moved by the Spirit to convey to present generations what the Spirit said to the churches in the past, and what he is saying to the churches now. His Introduction in this volume is an explanation of his point of view for interpreting The Revelation. His spirit is irenic toward others who may not fully agree with his conclusions. Study also The Outline before passing through the portals into the textual exposition.

When Dr. Erdman wrote this volume he was professor of practical theology in Princeton Seminary. Previously, and during a portion of his professorship, he held three pastorates, two in Philadelphia and one in Princeton. These experiences fitted the man to combine scholarly gifts with practical application of Biblical teachings. The seventeen commentaries appealed to church school teachers, study groups, pastors, college and seminary students, church librarians, and individual lay people for their own personal enrichment and spiritual education. The continuing demand necessitated numerous printings until the plates and type grew thin and broken with wear. To supply requests for the Erdman series this paperback edition is issued with entirely new plates and type.

Today's world has Christian witnesses on every continent, and on the islands of the seven seas. Many of these people are asking, "When the Son of man comes, will he find faith on earth?"

Their reading and understanding of The Revelation should fortify them to believe that ultimate victory belongs to God and his Christ.

EARL F. ZEIGLER

FOREWORD

This volume presents the text and an exposition of the last, and the most perplexing, book of the Bible. It is published with diffidence because of the difficulties and mysteries involved, with a plea for tolerance of divergent views, and yet with a deepening confidence in the practical and imperishable values of this portion of sacred Scripture. To it alone is attached the specific promise, "Blessed is he that readeth." Neither cold neglect nor heated controversy, neither skeptical criticism nor fanatical vagaries, have stopped its perennial springs of comfort and inspiration and hope. In vivid colors it pictures the inevitable triumph of right over wrong, the ultimate victory of truth and faith, and the final universal rule of the Prince of Peace. Yet it is not designed to encourage idle dreaming or sentimental speculation. It constitutes a call to sacrificial service, to courageous witness, and to valiant struggle, until "the kingdom of the world is become the kingdom of our Lord, and of his Christ."

INTRODUCTION

THE CHARACTER OF THE REVELATION

The Revelation of John is unique. Because of the intricacy of its literary structure, the splendor of its poetic imagery, the majestic scope of its inspired visions, the mystery of its cryptic symbols, and its dramatic presentation of eternal truths, this book is distinct in character from all other parts of the Bible.

It is regarded from the most contradictory points of view. To some persons it is fascinating; to others, forbidding. To some it is practical; to others, mystical. For some it is the subject of ceaseless study and confident exposition; for others it is an enigma from which they have turned in absolute despair.

Among those who continue to read the book there is, however, a remarkable agreement as to its substance and aim. All regard it as a book of consolation and cheer. They may differ as to the meaning of its details and the solution of its riddles, but all find it to be a message designed to encourage suffering and tempted followers of Christ by an assurance of their deliverance and the triumph of his cause.

It was written for those who were in danger of abandoning their faith, either because of present persecutions and impending disaster or because of the allurements of a godless world. They were reminded anew of the unseen presence and the future appearing of their Lord. They were called to fight against the forces of evil, yet only with the weapons of patient endurance and unswerving loyalty to Christ. They were to "overcome" as they followed in the train of their triumphant King. They were made to believe that to be on the side of Christ is to be on the side of ultimate victory. They were taught that the Golden

Age is not in the past but is yet to come. They were given the inspiring assurance that amid all the conflict of classes, the crash of empires, and the contradictions and testings of individual life, a divine purpose is being wrought out; that through the strife and the tumult draw ever nearer the supreme triumph of Christ and the perfected Kingdom of God.

This is a book of judgments and of doom. The darker side of the picture is never for a moment concealed. God is just. Sin must be punished. Impenitence and rebellion issue in misery and defeat. Here is no sentimental confusion of right and wrong. Here is no weak tolerance of evil. There is mention of "the Lamb that hath been slain," but also of "the wrath of the Lamb." There is a "river of water of life," but also a "lake of fire." Here is revealed a God of love who is to dwell among men, to wipe away all tears, and to abolish death and sorrow and pain; but first his enemies must be subdued. Indeed, The Revelation is in large measure a picture of the last great conflict between the forces of evil and the power of God. The colors are lurid and are borrowed from the convulsions of nature and from the scenes of human history, with their battles and their carnage. The struggle is titanic. Countless hordes of demonic warriors rise in opposition to him who is "King of Kings, and Lord of Lords." Upon them, "woes" are pronounced, "bowls" of wrath are poured out, and overwhelming destruction is visited. A brighter day is to come, but there is thunder before the dawn.

This is a book of poetry and of song. For this reason it has appealed to the master minds in the realms of literature and of music. As a whole it constitutes a majestic epic. Its spirit never can be caught, and its visions never can be understood, by a mind which moves only in the sphere of sober prose. Here celestial music is sounding, choirs of angels are singing, and "harpers harping with their harps," and we hear the hymns of the redeemed in glory. Some of the songs are pitched in a minor key. There are lamentations and threnodies, as well as hymns of triumph. Indeed, one of the most notable passages in the book is the lament over Babylon, as the kings and merchants and mariners "weap and mourn" over the fallen city . (Rev., ch. 18.)

However, the dominant note is that of praise. Such is the song of the seraphs: "Holy, holy, holy, is the Lord God, the Almighty, who was and who is and who is to come" (ch. 4:8). Such, too, is the "new song" addressed to the Lamb: "Worthy art thou . . . : for thou wast slain, and didst purchase unto God with thy blood men of every tribe, and tongue, and people, and nation, and madest them to be unto our God a kingdom and priests; and they reign upon the earth" (ch. 5:9-10). And such is the anthem of the angels: "Worthy is the Lamb that hath been slain to receive the power, and riches, and wisdom, and might, and honor, and glory, and bessing" (v. 12). Then there is the triumphant chorus of the elders: "We give thee thanks, O Lord God, the Almighty, who art and who wast; because thou hast taken thy great power, and didst reign" (ch. 11:17). There is also the fourfold chorus of hallelujahs, following the judgment upon Babylon and introducing the glorious appearing of Christ. (Ch. 19:1-8.)

Such are some of these inspired compositions which are classed among the most sublime passages in all the literature of the world.

This is a book of visions and of symbols. Excepting the opening and closing paragraphs, and the letters to the seven churches (chs. 2; 3), the rest of the book is composed wholly of visions which presented themselves to the mind of the enraptured prophet when under the influence of the divine Spirit. Nothing else is historical, nothing literal. The book is a series of pictures created in the imagination of the writer. They are not statements of events or formal expressions of doctrine. They are dramatic representations of truth which were visible only to the mind of the seer. They are thus mental images expressing objective realities.

With such visions all readers of the Bible are familiar. Some of those recorded elsewhere in Scripture were conveyed in the form of dreams; others came to men who were in a state of trance. Abraham had his vision when "a horror of great darkness fell upon him." Jacob caught his vision as he lay asleep at Beth-el. Balaam, even when desiring to curse Israel, saw

"the vision of the Almighty,
Falling down, and having his eyes open."

Large parts of the prophecies of Ezekiel and Zechariah are presented in similar forms. So, in the New Testament, Peter was in a trance, on the housetop at Joppa, when he saw the vision of the "sheet let down from heaven," and Paul, when writing of "visions and revelations," declared that he "was caught up into Paradise, and heard unspeakable words, which it is not lawful for a man to utter."

Such forms of communicating divine realities are more vivid and arresting than the more prosaic methods of teaching. They are far more impressive than the most elaborate verbal descriptions or the most logical processes of reasoning.

Furthermore, these visions were presented in the form of symbols. What the prophet saw were not actual persons or events to be remembered and recorded but rather images to be interpreted, and as such to be understood. The intention was to fix the thought, not upon the symbol, but upon the idea which the symbol was designed to represent. Such is Oriental symbolism. The images are not capable of pictorial representation. They are intended for the mind of a poet, not for the brush of a painter. To depict our Lord with a sword projecting from his mouth, to look for the appearance on earth of horses with "the heads of lions" and with "tails . . . like unto serpents," to conceive of the devil as bound with a metal chain is irreverent, grotesque, absurd. When, however, we think of the ideas which the symbols represent, then the visions which they form become vivid, instructive, real.

These symbols are borrowed from the Old Testament or are taken from familiar objects in nature. In fact, no book is so dependent upon the ancient Scripture for its interpretation as is The Revelation. The tree of life, the wilderness, the tabernacle, the Temple, Mt. Zion and the Holy City, Babylon and Magog, angels and seraphim, the golden candlesticks and the Ark of the Covenant—these and numberless other images make the message plain and forcible to those who are acquainted with the histories and prophecies of Israel.

Quite as familiar are the natural objects and phenomena which lend color to these inspired visions. The sky, the sun, the sea, earthquake and thunder, lightning and falling stars, rivers and mountains and trees—all have their appropriate places in the scenes of terror sketched by the writer to convey his message concerning things spiritual and ideal.

The use of these symbols is uniform. However difficult to interpret, they are not used so as to contradict and confuse. They form a language of their own. Babylon, the beast, the Holy City, the sea, trumpets, seals, and bowls—all have a fixed and consistent meaning.

This likewise is true of the use of numbers. They form an important feature in the symbolism of the book. They are not used without design, but with a uniform significance. The number 4, or the number 7, or the numbers 12 and 1000, as examples, are not to be interpreted literally, but as the world number, the number of totality, the number of completeness, and the number of superlative greatness.

Last of all, it may be suggested that the symbols of The

Revelation, and the visions they compose, are obviously complex. They are made up of many features. However, it must not be supposed that a meaning must be found for each minute detail. As in the parables of our Lord, the main idea in each case must be sought. The attempt must be made to interpret the symbol or the vision as a whole. The details may deepen the impression, but they must not be allowed to divert the thought. When properly understood, such picturesque and symbolic vehicles of truth are a most valuable means of conveying conceptions to the human mind.

This is a book of prophecy. So the writer repeatedly affirms. He refers to "the words of the book of this prophecy" and again and again to "the words of the prophecy of this book." Furthermore, he uses the word "prophecy" in the specific sense of prediction. It is true that a "prophet" usually occupied a wider sphere. He spoke for God, and his messages might relate to the present or to the past. This writer, however, was concerned particularly with the future. He was revealing "the things which must shortly come to pass." He spoke not only of "the things which are," but chiefly of "the things which shall come to pass hereafter." Whether these "things" referred to events in the days of imperial Rome, or to events of the present era, or to such as will transpire at "the end of the age," they were regarded by the writer as belonging to the future, however near to him that future may have seemed.

Still further, The Revelation is classified as related to one particular kind of prophecy known as "apocalyptic." Just because it is in the form of visions and symbols, as already noted, it might be regarded as an "apocalypse." Yet its substance is quite as truly apocalyptic as is its form; for writings of this class were designed to comfort the people of God under persecution. They dealt with the evil character of the present age and the opposition of the world powers to the will of God. They pointed to deliverance, not in any process of development, but in a divine intervention. They predicted the coming of Christ, the judgment, and the dawning of a new age.

Yet The Revelation differs widely from all other apocalyptic writings. So distinct is its character that a question might be raised as to whether or not it is classified properly as an apocalypse. Those writings appeared under false names. They were crude, confused, unedifying, and often absurd. They evidently were the products of unbridled fancy. On the other hand, The Revelation is orderly, dignified, serious, purposeful, sublime. At the least it is supreme among all apocalyptic productions, and therefore rightfully called the "Apocalypse." It is not a book of human fantasies. It is a true prophecy inspired of God.

This is a book of practical and permanent moral and spiritual values. It has kept its place in the New Testament, and it holds the affection of countless readers, not because of the mystery of its symbols or the intricacy of its literary form or the encouragement of its predictions, but rather because of its embodiment of the great essentials of our Christian faith. Set forth in its symbols, and emphasized by its visions, are those verities which form the substance of revealed truth. Here God is revealed in his divine majesty, in his holiness, in his justice, in his omnipotence, and in his love. Christ appears as the Prophet, Priest, and King. He is at once a character in human history and also the eternal Son of God. He is "the Lamb that hath been slain," but he secures universal triumph by his death, and he holds in his pierced hands the destinies of the world. One with the Father and the Son is the Eternal Spirit in his sevenfold, ceaseless ministry.

Here sin is depicted in its most satanic forms and with its inevitable penalty and doom. Here man appears, free, responsible, immortal, created for fellowship with God.

Here the picture of a "Paradise Lost" is replaced by the
matchless vision of a "Paradise Regained." This is a
book intended to establish the faith and support the hope
of a persecuted and imperiled church. It continues to this
day as a precious compendium of Christian truth and an
unfailing inspiration to lives of holiness and courage and
of unconquerable trust in God.

AUTHORSHIP AND DATE

The Revelation was written by the apostle John during
the reign of the Roman emperor Domitian, about the year
A.D. 96. Such at least is the earliest tradition and such
the conclusion of most recent scholarship. There are, indeed, other variant views which are deserving of serious
thought. Some writers even are insisting that the authorship of this book is composite, and that an original Jewish
apocalypse was rewritten, with certain Christian features
added by a later hand. Most students, however, discover
in The Revelation a perfect unity which can be attributed
only to a single mind.

The author calls himself John, both in the opening and
the closing verses of the book. He states that because of
his Christian faith he has been banished to the isle of
Patmos. He addresses the churches of Asia with a consciousness of unquestioned authority. Of no other person
in the first century could these statements be made. The
conjecture that the book was composed by a more or less
mythical "John the Presbyter" has been practically abandoned, and there is an increasing consensus of belief that
The Revelation was written by none other than "the dis-
ciple whom Jesus loved."

The objections to this view consist largely in certain al-
leged contrasts between The Revelation and the Fourth
Gospel. It is true that there are differences of style and
expression and literary form. Yet there are, on the other
hand, many points of striking agreement. The diction is

said not to be the same; but what other writer so characteristically described our Lord as the "Word," and the "Lamb"? Who else unites so closely the death and resurrection of Christ, or so uses the verbs "witness," "tabernacle," "keep," "overcome," or so refers to "living water," to "manna," to the "shepherd" and the "sheep"?

The lurid, thunderous passages of the Apocalypse are said to preclude the authorship of the meditative, mystical John, "the apostle of love"; but it must not be forgotten that he was also a son "of thunder," who wished to call down fire from heaven, who declared himself able to endure the baptism of martyrdom, and sought for himself a chief place in the glorious Kingdom of Christ.

When all the evidence has been weighed there is no sufficient reason for abandoning the ancient belief that The Revelation was written by the apostle who at the Last Supper reclined "in Jesus' bosom," the apostle who ever "beheld his glory, glory as of the only begotten from the Father."

As to the date of the composition, some scholars, particularly of the last century, have been inclined to assign The Revelation, either wholly or in part, to the reign of Nero, and to the year A.D. 68. There were two main arguments. The first was the reference to "the holy city" (ch. 11), which was taken to imply that the book was written before the destruction of Jerusalem. The second was the supposed identity of Nero with the "beast" (ch. 13).

As to the first, if the predicted preservation of "the temple of God" and "the altar" and the destruction of "the holy city" are literal references to Jerusalem, as this argument requires, then the prediction was falsified by the event; for when the city fell the Temple was not preserved but shared in the tragic disaster and ruin. Since such a contradiction is inconsistent with inspiration, this position has been generally abandoned, and the references to the holy city are now interpreted symbolically in accordance with the unquestionably figurative character of the entire chapter. Furthermore, the long description of the New Jerusalem (chs. 21; 22) implies that the ancient city already had been destroyed, and that in its place a new and heavenly city was in the mind of John.

As to the "beast," which was actually killed and restored to life, it has been found increasingly difficult to adapt the description to the historic character Nero; and modern scholars, in considering Nero, are less inclined to accept the fanciful interpretation of "Six hundred and sixty and six" as "the number" of his name.

It is far more probable that The Revelation was written in A.D. 96, the last year of the reign of the Roman emperor Domitian. Many facts point to this conclusion. First of all, there is the almost unanimous testimony of the church fathers, from the second century through the first half of the fifth century. During this long era, and in all parts of the Christian church, it was firmly believed that the visions of John were to be assigned to the days of Domitian and not of Nero.

Then again, modern historians agree that the Neronian persecution hardly extended beyond the city of Rome, while the persecution under Domitian was spread widely over the empire.

Furthermore, the persecution under Nero was not on the grounds of religious belief. He wished to avert from himself suspicion of the crime of having burned the city, and therefore attempted to implicate the new sect called "Christians." This was in A.D. 64, and there is no proof that his fiendish cruelties to the infant church continued until or during the year A.D. 68. On the contrary, the martyrdoms under Domitian were due to a refusal on the part of Christians to worship the emperor as divine, or, as John declares, to "worship the image of the beast." The ground of persecution, therefore, indicates the reign of Domitian and not that of Nero.

Nor did the means of punishment adopted by Nero include banishment. There was imprisonment, torture, drenching with oil and then burning the wretched victims as torches, and crucifixion; but exile is not mentioned. On the other hand, there are detailed stories and references to a general policy of banishment as employed by Domitian.

One other fact is worthy of mention. The state of the churches established by Paul in "Asia," and described by John in The Revelation, was such as to have required a much longer period of development than the earlier date would allow. For example, the church at Smyrna was not founded until A.D. 64.

For these and other reasons, there is now rather general agreement upon the later date for the composition of The Revelation.

To ascertain the exact time when John, as a Christian martyr on the isle of Patmos, received his visions is a matter of real concern, for both the inspiration and the correct interpretation of the Apocalypse are involved. However, it is of still greater importance to note the character of the time in which the book was composed. It was in days when the church was in great suffering and peril. The allurements of the world or the fear of pain and loss were threatening to make men disloyal to their divine Lord. A godless state and a pagan religion were leagued together to destroy the cause of Christ. Dangers even more dark and dread were on the horizon. Deliverance by no human power was possible. It was in a time like this that John caught those inspiring visions of the returning, triumphant King, of his universal reign, and of the celestial city established upon earth, which have been the source of inspiration, of comfort, and of hope in all ages of the world.

THE INTERPRETATION

The main message of the Apocalypse is perfectly plain. As to its meaning all readers agree. It presents to the troubled and distressed an assurance of the ultimate triumph of Christ and the eternal blessedness of all who put their trust in him. One almost could wish that nothing further need be attempted in the way of interpreting the book. It surely is to be regretted that this essential message often is lost by those who center their thought on unsolved mysteries of detail. Such readers are like voyagers who are caught in eddies and fail to appreciate the majestic sweep of the main stream.

There are others who enjoy the opening and closing chapters of The Revelation, but feel that no effort should be made to interpret the great central section of the prophecy. There is no question that these favorite chapters are the more easily understood and are of more practical and universal value. The first three chapters contain moral and religious instruction for the church of all ages; the fourth and fifth present the work of the Redeemer by which salvation has been secured; and the last two depict the celestial glories in which salvation is to be complete.

However, during the Christian centuries the church has felt that some definite meaning should be assigned to all parts of the book, and that even its most mysterious visions lend emphasis to its central message. The theories of interpretation have been many and they have been widely divergent. They have been classified commonly as: the "preterist," the "historical," the "futurist," and the "spiritual." The division is not exact. Different views often are united in whole or in part. In each view there are elements of undoubted truth. Each is defended by scholars whose ability and piety are unquestioned. Probably each will contribute something to the ultimate solution of those problems which at present appear so difficult and baffling.

The "preterist" view regards the visions of the book as referring chiefly, if not exclusively, to events which are past. These events belonged to the age of the writer. They concerned the Roman persecution of Christians and predicted the fall of the empire. To most of these interpreters Nero was the "beast," and "Babylon" was imperial Rome. In this view there is much of truth. There can be no doubt that the writer was addressing Christians of his own day, and first had in view conditions and circumstances which were familiar to his readers. Such is the case with all inspired prophecy. The seer looks upon conditions which confront his own people. He gives messages adapted to their needs and intended for their present encouragement and relief. However, such an interpretation by no means exhausts the meaning of The Revelation. The knowledge of ancient history does throw light upon the book; but the more accurate that knowledge, the more it reveals the fact that there are few points of agreement between the visions of John and the annals of imperial Rome. Undoubtedly there are continual references to emperor worship and to the persecuting power of Rome. Both the city and the state are evidently in the mind of the writer. The circumstances of his own day give him the occasion and the background of his message. Yet it is difficult, if not actually impossible, to discover in the pages of the Apocalypse the description of any specific incidents of ancient history. The vision of the writer is turned toward the future. The events he pictures cannot be confined to the first century. He sees a struggle which is age-long. He describes a victory which will be made complete only by the reappearing of Christ.

So it is with the "historical" interpretation of The Revelation. It also contains elements of truth, but it has led its advocates into obvious and serious errors. According to this view, the Apocalypse contains visions which reveal in advance outstanding movements and events in human history from the days of Rome to the end of the world. Here are discovered, for example, the invasion of the barbarians, the Protestant Reformation, the French Revolution, the World War. The "beast" is understood to represent Muhammad, or Luther, or Napoleon, or some modern dictator. Advocates of this view confidently endeavor to find in modern political history the fulfillment of the prophecies of John. They have united quite commonly in declaring that the "beast," or Antichrist, is the Pope, and "Babylon" is papal Rome. Then, by adding to the date of the rise of the papacy the number 1260, which measures the career of the "beast," they have sought to determine the year of our Lord's return.

The failure of this last prediction and the absurdities of these interpretations have brought prophetic study into disrepute. However, it is true that many world movements and historical events have illustrated principles and been the same in kind as those set forth in The Revelation, and there can be no doubt that the seer did sweep the whole horizon of the future. He began with the persecuting power of Rome and he looks forward to the last great conflict between the world power and Christ.

Therefore, there must be much of truth also in the interpretation known as the "futurist." This view confines the visions of The Revelation to events immediately connected with the return of the Lord. In its extreme form it holds that even the letters to the seven churches are designed for an age still future. Its more moderate advocates teach that directly after the record of these letters the church must be understood to be caught away by a "secret rapture," and chapters 4 to 19 of The Revelation refer wholly to the experiences of the Jews and the career of the "beast" under whom they suffer during "the great tribulation." According to this view, Christ returns to destroy the "beast," to bind Satan, and to introduce on earth his reign of a thousand years.

Such theories have been of service to the church in at least turning the thought toward the Second Coming of Christ. This is undoubtedly the great event toward which all the predictions of The Revelation point. This is the focus around which all its teachings revolve. Therefore it is unfortunate that so many advocates of this view have lost sight of the circumstances which led John to write his "prophecy"; that they have yielded to a servile literalism, and yet, on the other hand, have introduced so much material that is purely imaginary and fanciful; that they find so few references to the church, and so little that is intended to meet the needs of believers during these passing centuries. They do emphasize, however, the truth of the Lord's return, which they find set forth in ch. 19. This view is thus of boundless benefit to the church as it has magnified and exalted "the blessed hope" of the personal and glorious appearing of Christ.

The "spiritual," or "poetic" or "ideal," theory of interpretation of the Apocalypse finds in this book no reference to specific events or persons of the past or present or future, but only the presentation of great spiritual principles, intended to guide and encourage the followers of Christ through all the ages of the world. These principles are illustrated by the successive symbolic visions. They reach their climax in the great reality that right ultimately conquers wrong, that God is the moral Ruler of the universe, that Christ is to triumph over all his enemies, that the world is moving on, even through tragedy and disaster, to its age of gold.

It can hardly be denied that this theory is often presented in forms which are rather superficial and sentimental. It evades the interpretation of difficult passages. It raises the fair question of why such elaborate imagery is employed through so long a series of visions to illustrate principles which have been so plainly set forth in other books of the Bible; and furthermore, it may be asked, do not principles become even more impressive when embodied in events which the writer saw, and in still more momentous events which in prophetic vision he beheld on the horizon of a brighter era which was yet to dawn?

At least this spiritual theory warns us against a too crass view of prophecy as being, in too literal a sense, "history written in advance." It cautions us against looking in the

Apocalypse for a detailed outline of the future. The writer is not picturing the rise of the papacy, nor the career of Muhammad, nor details of a future Antichrist as to his origin, his name, his time, or the exact character of his doom. He is presenting, in symbolic form, typical events which do not minutely predict but which illustrate the conflict between Satan and the Savior, between the world power and the church. This conflict reaches its climax in the appearance of a man of sin, in his overthrow by the victorious Christ, and in the appearing of "a new heaven and a new earth," when the tabernacle of God will be with men.

The mere mention of such diverse theories, each one held by scholars of keen intelligence and unquestioned sincerity, indicates how much of modesty and charity should be manifested by anyone who attempts an exposition of this inspired prophecy. It cannot be denied that its discussion has been attended frequently by signs of irritation and temper. Charges of ignorance and even impiety have been made against the most earnest and devout students. Probably the consideration of no book requires so much humility, so much patience, so much prayer. Possibly the careful consideration of none other will afford more of comfort, of cheer, and of hope. One who reads the book, and is familiar with its many interpretations, realizes fully that "we know in part, and we prophesy in part." There is encouragement, however, in the belief that "when that which is perfect is come" we shall "know fully even as also [we have been] . . . fully known."

THE STRUCTURE

The literary structure of The Revelation is intricate and interesting. It is also important. Indeed, it may be maintained that the right interpretation of the book depends in large measure upon a knowledge of its structure.

Evidently the outline was determined by the use of numbers. The number seven is formative, as are its component numbers, three and four. In addition to a prologue and an epilogue, the book seems to consist of seven parts, and in most of these parts there are seven subdivisions or special features. There are the seven letters to churches in the province of Asia, followed by the opening of seven seals and the sounding of seven trumpets; after an intermediate section depicting the conflict between Christ and his adversaries, seven vials, or bowls, of judgment are poured out. This section is followed by a description of the final doom of Christ's enemies, and the book closes with a picture of "a new heaven and a new earth," and particularly of the New Jerusalem.

Then, again, in each division of sevens there is a distinction between the first three and the last four, or between the first four and the last three. Again, each of the seven divisions of the book is opened with an introductory vision vitally related to the subject matter which follows. Furthermore, in the case of the seven seals, the seven trumpets, the central section of conflict, the seven bowls, and possibly in the section which follows, the series of sevens, or the prophetic vision, is interrupted by a parenthetic episode, or interlude. These episodes are in the nature of consolation and cheer for the people of God while the scenes of catastrophe or judgment are unfolding.

Another feature to be noted is that the visions are not presented as following successively in the order of time. There is repetition and review. The scenes depicted are parallel, at least in part. Thus the sixth seal seems to reach the very end of the age; but with the opening of the seventh seal there is a pause, and the seven trumpets go back in time to the events under a portion of the earlier seals. The sixth trumpet seems to sound the note of final victory and to usher in the return of Christ. Yet again there is a delay. New series of events are introduced.

So when the seventh bowl is poured out, a great voice

is heard, saying, "It is done," and for a third time the very end of the dispensation has been reached; yet again the thought is turned back, and the dooms upon Christ's enemies are successively recorded, until at last he appears in triumph.

The method is evidently that of review. Yet the visions are not presented as revealing events which are wholly parallel. The seals concern only one fourth of the earth; the trumpets, one third; while the bowls are total in their effect. Thus, while there is recapitulation, it is in the form of climax. The series do not all begin at the same point, but all lead on to the same end and goal. Events of the same kind are pictured, but each series of judgments is more dread in its character, more terrible in its results. Each repetition adds color and the impressiveness of detail.

In fact, contrast and repetition and climax are evident features in the literary structure of the book. However, the most conspicuous feature is that of symmetry. Each of the letters to the seven churches follows the same exact literary scheme. All seven form a section descriptive of the church in its present imperfection and peril. With these chapters the book opens, and, with poetic balance, it closes with the picture of the New Jerusalem, in the two chapters containing the vision of the church, perfect and glorious.

In the five central sections there is the same harmonious and artistic order. Two sections, those of the seals and the trumpets, depict revolution and catastrophe, out of which naturally emerge the great antagonists whose conflict forms the central point of the dramatic action, while the two sections of bowls and dooms paint vividly the destruction of Christ's enemies and prepare for the closing picture of his perfected church in the splendor of the "new earth."

These and similar features of this balanced and rhythmic structure become apparent as one traces in order the course of the prophetic visions.

The prologue (ch. 1:1-8) sets forth the source and destination of The Revelation. The risen Christ is sending his message to the seven churches in the province of Asia. The first vision, which immediately follows (vs. 9-20), reveals Christ in the midst of the churches, ready to correct, to sustain, to punish or reward. This vision is introductory to the whole book, and particularly to the seven letters which are here recorded (chs. 2; 3).

The opening of the seven seals (chs. 6:1 to 8:1) is preceded by a vision in heaven (chs. 4; 5). Here Christ appears in the place of supreme power. In his hand the almighty Creator is placing the seven-sealed book containing the destinies of the world.

As six successive seals are broken, there follow scenes of peace and war and famine and death and martyrdom and catastrophe, such as were to attend the church in its mission through the ages. (Ch. 6.) However, the first parenthetic vision (ch. 7) reveals the people of God as safe amid all disaster, whether sealed on earth or with the whiterobed throng in heaven.

The opening of the seventh seal is attended by a brief period of silence. Then appears the vision of an angel, who at the golden altar is mingling the incense of heaven with the prayers of the saints. This vision is preparatory to the sounding of the seven trumpets, for it is in answer to these prayers that the events announced by the trumpets take place. (Ch. 8:1-6.)

At the sounding of the first four trumpets, plagues are visited on a third part of the earth and of the sea and of the fountains and of the rivers of water, while a third part of the sun, the moon, and the stars is darkened. (Vs. 7-13.) As the fifth trumpet sounds, swarms of demonic beings, in the form of locusts, pour forth from "the abyss" under Apollyon, their king, and for five months inflict torment on all men who do not have "the seal of God." (Ch. 9:1-12.)

The sixth trumpet is the signal for the appearing of vast

armies of horsemen from the region of the Euphrates. They have power to destroy one third of mankind. Yet in spite of these plagues and destruction the rest of mankind do not repent. (Vs. 13-21.)

Between the sixth and seventh trumpets, as between the sixth and seventh seals, is introduced an episode or parenthetic vision. An angel appears who gives to the prophet an open booklet. When this has been eaten, it is revealed that Jerusalem, except the Temple and its inner court, is to be trodden down by the Gentiles for forty-two months. "Two witnesses" are to prophesy during that time; they are to be killed, and after three and a half days are to be raised to heaven. (Chs. 10:1 to 11:14.)

As the seventh trumpet sounds, heavenly voices announce the great consummation, the perfected "kingdom of our Lord, and of his Christ." (Vs. 15-19.)

The central section of the book (chs. 12 to 14) pictures the conflict between God and Satan, between the church and the world power. The introductory vision (ch. 12) shows the endeavor of Satan to destroy Christ at his birth, Satan's fall from heaven, and his persecution of the people of God.

The main feature, however, of this central section is the universal rule of "a beast" who rises out of the sea and is empowered by Satan. Aided by a second beast rising out of the land, he attempts to kill all who do not bear his mark and who will not worship his image. (Ch. 13.)

A parenthetic episode (ch. 14:1-13) is introduced to comfort the people of God by assuring them of their safety and of the destruction of their enemies. There appears a vision of 144,000 of the redeemed, standing on Mt. Zion in company with the Lamb. (Vs. 1-5.) The voices of angels are heard proclaiming "eternal good tidings," also the destruction of Babylon, the doom of all who worship the beast, and the blessedness of martyrs. (Vs. 6-13.)

The consummation of this central vision is reached in

the picture of the harvest, when Christ gathers his sheaves into the garner, and of the vintage, when he treads down his foes in the wine press of his wrath. (Vs. 14-20.)

The vision of the seven bowls, or vials (ch. 16), is prefaced by an introductory vision (ch. 15) in which appear the redeemed singing by the "sea of glass," and in the heavenly temple, the seven angels having the seven last plagues.

As six angels pour out their bowls of wrath, dread judgments fall, affecting the earth, the sea, and the river Euphrates. (Ch. 16:1-12.)

Before the seventh bowl is poured out, there is introduced an episode (vs. 13-16) in which three demonic spirits are seen gathering all the kings of the world to the battle of Har-Magedon, or Armageddon.

At the pouring out of the seventh bowl, storm and earthquake and thunder burst forth, which accompany the final judgments of God upon his enemies. (Vs. 17-21.) These judgments are described in detail in the visions which immediately follow.

The visions of doom upon all the enemies of Christ (chs. 17 to 20) are opened by the preparatory vision of "Babylon the great" seated on "a scarlet-colored beast," but subsequently overthrown by the beast and his allies, who in turn are overcome by the "Lamb," called also "Lord of lords, and King of kings." (Ch. 17.)

The doom of "Babylon," because of the persecution of prophets and saints, is announced by an angel voice, and kings and merchants and mariners are heard lamenting the fall of the great city. (Ch. 18.)

After an interlude, or episode, in which two hallelujahs celebrate the fall of Babylon and two announce "the marriage supper of the Lamb" (ch. 19:1-10), Christ is seen appearing as a victorious warrior, triumphing over his enemies, who are cast into "the lake of fire" (vs. 11-21).

The binding of Satan is followed by "a thousand years" of peace while risen martyrs reign with Christ. (Ch.

20:1-6.) Satan is loosed and leads the nations in a final assault against "the beloved city." The armies are consumed by fire from heaven and Satan is "cast into the lake of fire." (Vs. 7-10.) Then follows the description of the resurrection and the judgment of the dead. (Vs. 11-15.)

In the closing vision, the New Jerusalem is seen descending from heaven (ch. 21:1-8), and a description is given of the glory and the blessedness of this celestial city (chs. 21:9 to 22:5).

The epilogue consists of attestations to the divine trustworthiness and sanctity of the book and to the imminence of the events it describes. (Ch. 22:6-21.)

THE OUTLINE

III

I
THE PROLOGUE
Rev. 1:1-8

A. THE INSCRIPTION   Ch. 1:1-3

1 The Revelation of Jesus Christ, which God gave him to show unto his servants, even the things which must shortly come to pass: and he sent and signified it by his angel unto his servant John; 2 who bare witness of the word of God, and of the testimony of Jesus Christ, even of all things that he saw. 3 Blessed is he that readeth, and they that hear the words of the prophecy, and keep the things that are written therein: for the time is at hand.

The second word of The Revelation of John, in harmony with its opening verses, sounds a note of encouragement to all who attempt to read this difficult book. "Revelation," or the Greek word ἀποκάλυψις, which it translates, means "an unveiling," "a disclosure," "an apocalypse." The book was not intended to be a puzzle, a mystery, or an enigma which no one could solve. The writer expected his message to be understood. It was to bring to light realities which had been concealed. It was to impart truth which otherwise would have remained unknown.

It is, furthermore, encouraging to be assured that this Revelation, or Apocalypse, came from Christ. It not only is about him but it is from him. It is "the Revelation of Jesus Christ, which God gave him to show unto his servants." Thus the ultimate source is the Father. Two other agents are mentioned, by whom the divine message was finally brought to the servants of Christ: one is an "angel"; the other is the apostle John: "He sent and signified it by his angel unto his servant John." Thus the message came from the Father to the Son, and from the Son, through the ministry of an angel, to John, "who bare witness of the word of God, and of the testimony of Jesus Christ."

This message which John gave was communicated to him in the form of visions. It consisted of "all the things that he saw." It was in the nature of prophecy, for it concerned the "things which must shortly come to pass." Prophecy must always be difficult to interpret; and visions like those of John, which are clothed in Oriental symbols and molded by circumstances of his own day, necessarily present problems and embody mysteries. Nevertheless the servants of Christ should expect to find light and leading in the pages of his Revelation. Indeed, they are encouraged more specifically by a definite assurance: "Blessed is he that readeth, and they that hear the words of the prophecy, and keep the things that are written therein: for the time is at hand."

This is the first of seven beatitudes which are recorded in the book (chs. 1:3; 14:13; 16:15; 19:9; 20:6; 22:7, 14). It is addressed, first of all, to the member of an early Christian assembly who read aloud the book to those who were present. He and his hearers were to expect a divine blessing. Yet it is implied that the same blessing may be expected by all who will fulfill the condition which is named, and will "keep the things that are written." The commandments of the book must be obeyed. Its fulfillment must be expected if its benefits are to be received. It is not a book of mere prediction. Its moral instruction must be heeded. However, its effect is dependent on the belief that the season for the fulfillment of its prophecies is near: "The time is at hand."

Thus read, the book is of practical helpfulness and of ethical value. It is not designed to satisfy curiosity, but to stimulate courage and steadfastness as well as hope. Its very inscription presents the messages which follow as subjects for the private study and the public instruction of the Christian church.

B. THE SALUTATION   Ch. 1:4-8

4 John to the seven churches that are in Asia: Grace to you and peace, from him who is and who was and who is to come; and from the seven Spirits that are before his throne; 5 and from Jesus Christ, who is the faithful witness, the firstborn of the dead, and the ruler of the kings of the earth. Unto him that loveth us, and loosed us from our sins by his blood; 6 and he made us to be a kingdom, to be priests unto his God and Father; to him be the glory and the dominion for ever and ever. Amen. 7 Behold, he cometh with the clouds; and every eye shall see him, and they that pierced him; and all the tribes of the earth shall mourn over him. Even so, Amen.

8 I am the Alpha and the Omega, saith the Lord God, who is and who was and who is to come, the Almighty.

The inscription (vs. 1-3) has set forth the divine source, the prophetic character, and the blessed purpose of The Revelation. Then follows the salutation, in which the writer, John, addresses "the seven churches that are in Asia." The salutation thus indicates that the entire book, and not merely the portion containing the seven letters (chs. 2; 3), is intended for the churches of Asia. This "Asia" does not refer to the continent of that name, nor to Asia Minor, but only to the small Roman province of which Ephesus was the capital. The fact that in this province there were other Christian churches besides those named by John (ch. 1:11) indicates that the number seven is used as a symbol. It was the sacred and complete number. The seven churches were representative of the whole church in all the world and in all ages. Thus John is addressing the entire book to the church universal.

The salutation follows the form usual in the New Testament epistles. It consists, in substance, of a prayer for the divine gifts of "grace" and "peace." These gifts are besought from the Father, from the Holy Spirit, and from the Son, Jesus Christ. The Father is described in terms of his eternal being as "him who is and who was and who is to come." The Holy Spirit, in view of his perfect and complete operation and energy, is symbolized as "the seven Spirits that are before his throne." Jesus Christ is presented in the character in which he appears in this book, as "the faithful witness, the firstborn of the dead, and the ruler of the kings of the earth." The thought is centered upon Christ; and the mention of his redeeming work calls forth from the heart of the writer this doxology of praise: "Unto him that loveth us, and loosed us from our sins by his blood; and he made us to be a kingdom, to be priests unto his God and Father; to him be the glory and the dominion for ever and ever. Amen." The infinite love of Christ is shown in the fact that he died for us. This sacrificial death has secured not only cleansing but also freedom from the power of sin. Furthermore, it has brought us into a position of glorious privilege: "He made us to be a kingdom, to be priests unto his God." The Revelation represents the church as the true Israel. Through faith in Christ, believers of every race possess those rights which in type belonged to the Jewish nation. "Ye are an elect race," writes Peter, "a royal priesthood, a holy nation, a people for God's own possession." So, in The Revelation, the apostle John declares that, in virtue of its relation to Christ, the church has a royal standing. It is "a kingdom." Believers reign, or will reign, with Christ over the world; and in virtue of his atoning death they enjoy the right of continual priestly access to God. To such privileges grave responsibilities are related. Since we belong to the Kingdom of God which is to be as perfect on earth as it is now in heaven, we are to watch and work and pray for its coming. Since we are priests, we should be offering continually the sacrifices of praise and of self-denial and of loving ministry, pouring out our lives in intercession and in sympathetic service of our fellowmen.

Grateful devotion to Christ, which gives birth to this doxology, is the motive for action which breathes through all the chapters of this book. This devotion to his Lord carries the thought of the writer forward to the time when Christ will appear in kingly glory. It is as though he were continuing his doxology when he exclaims: "Behold, he cometh with the clouds; and every eye shall see him, and they that pierced him; and all the tribes of the earth shall mourn over him. Even so, Amen."

This coming of Christ for the establishment of the perfected Kingdom of God is the great central theme of the book. It is not fulfilled alone in the movement by which the purposes of God are being wrought out on the stage of history. There is not only this divine process; there is also a final crisis. The return of Christ is not to be interpreted as an evolution; it points to an event. There is to be an actual, personal, visible reappearance of our risen and ascended Lord. Of that event, there are phases which are blessed and full of comfort and hope. As portrayed here, however, it is a coming in judgment. There is no mention of repentance or of faith on the part either of the Jews who once rejected him or of the Gentile nations who have refused to obey him. Here they see him in whom they have not believed; here the mourning is in despair. This is an announcement of the last scene in which the judgments predicted in this book reach their climax, and when by the defeat of his enemies Christ establishes his universal rule.

To this solemn prophecy, containing the main burden of his message, the writer adds the authority of the divine name: "I am the Alpha and the Omega, saith the Lord God, who is and who was and who is to come, the Almighty." Only here and in ch. 21:5 is God represented as the Speaker. "The Alpha and the Omega," the first and last letters of the Greek alphabet, are mentioned to denote, not the eternity of God, but his all-inclusive power. He is "the Almighty." He has controlled the events which culminate in the Advent. That event too is in his power, as will be that new order, "a new heaven and a new earth," which the return of Christ will introduce.

II
THE SEVEN VISIONS
Chs. 1:9 to 22:5

A. THE SEVEN LETTERS TO THE CHURCHES OF ASIA   Chs. 1:9 to 3:22

1. INTRODUCTORY VISION: CHRIST AMONG THE CHURCHES   Ch. 1:9-20

9 I John, your brother and partaker with you in the tribulation and kingdom and patience which are in Jesus, was in the isle that is called Patmos, for the word of God and the testimony of Jesus. 10 I was in the Spirit on the Lord's day, and I heard behind me a great voice, as of a trumpet 11 saying, What thou seest, write in a book and send it to the seven churches: unto Ephesus, and unto Smyrna, and unto Pergamum, and unto Thyatira, and unto Sardis, and unto Philadelphia, and unto Laodicea. 12 And I turned to see the voice that spake with me. And having turned I saw seven golden candlesticks; 13 and in the midst of the candlesticks one like unto a son of man, clothed with a garment down to the foot, and girt about at the breasts with a golden girdle. 14 And his head and his hair were white as white wool, white as snow; and his eyes were as a flame of fire; 15 and his feet like unto burnished brass, as if it had been refined in a furnace; and his voice as the voice of many waters. 16 And he had in his right hand seven stars: and out of his mouth proceeded a sharp two-edged sword: and his countenance was as the sun shineth in his strength. 17 And when I saw him, I fell at his feet as one dead. And he laid his right hand upon me, saying, Fear not; I am the first and the last, 18 and the Living one; and I was dead, and behold, I am alive for evermore, and I have the keys of death and of Hades. 19 Write therefore the things which thou sawest, and the things which are, and the things which shall come to pass hereafter; 20 the mys-

*tery of the seven stars which thou sawest in my right hand,
and the seven golden candlesticks. The seven stars are the
angels of the seven churches: and the seven candlesticks are
seven churches.*

The seven letters to the Asian churches form an integral
part, indeed the fundamental part, of the Apocalypse. All
its following visions depend for their significance upon
what these letters disclose. They give a picture of the
universal church, with the trials and triumphs of which
the rest of the book is concerned. They note the virtues
which must be manifested, the imperfections which must
be removed, the faith which must be maintained, if the
church is to prove victorious and is to share the ultimate
glory of her divine Lord. Most important of all, the
church must be reminded and assured that this Lord is an
abiding, personal Presence. The church must live as in
his constant sight, and must trust in his unfailing power.
It is for this reason that the letters are preceded and the
whole book is opened by an introductory vision in which
Christ is pictured as abiding in the midst of the church.

The circumstances under which the vision, and so the
whole Revelation, is given are so described as to indicate
how vitally related to his readers the prophet regarded
himself to be. He declares himself to be their "brother"
in the family of believers, and their fellow partaker "in the
tribulation and kingdom and patience which are in Jesus."
As some day they are to share the full glory of the Kingdom, so now they are sharing the sufferings and also the
steadfastness which the Christian life involves. John dis-
closes that he is an exile on the island of Patmos. This
barren, rocky, sun-scorched prison stood in the Aegean
Sea some seventy miles southwest of Ephesus. John is
suffering for the witness he has borne to the gospel message, or "for the word of God and the testimony of Jesus."

It is the Christian Sabbath, "the Lord's day." Possibly
the aged apostle has been thinking longingly of his dear

friends in the cities of Asia, across the sea, gathering in
their accustomed places of worship. Suddenly he is seized
with a spiritual ecstasy. He hears behind him "a great
voice, as of a trumpet." He turns and is overwhelmed by
a vision of his living Lord.

The voice bids him to "write in a book" all the revelations which are to follow and to send it to the churches of
Ephesus, Smyrna, Pergamum, Thyatira, Sardis, Philadelphia, and Laodicea. The order in which the cities are
named is that in which a messenger naturally might be
sent, as he followed the great circular road that bound together the most populous and influential part of the province. Ephesus, the chief city and capital, naturally is mentioned first; then Smyrna, located about forty miles to
the north; then Pergamum, some fifty miles farther north-
east; then Thyatira, about forty miles southeast; then
Sardis, thirty miles farther south; and Philadelphia and
Laodicea, about thirty and seventy miles to the southeast
of Sardis.

There were other Christian churches in Asia. That
only seven are selected indicates that these are symbolic of
the church universal. Some readers suppose that they
represent seven historic stages of this universal church.
Ephesus is said to be the church of the apostolic age;
Smyrna, the church of the Roman persecutions; Pergamum, of the age of Constantine; Thyatira, of the Middle
Ages; Sardis, of the Reformation period; Philadelphia, of
the present day; and Laodicea, the church of the last days.
Such suppositions are fanciful and quite aside from the
purpose of the prophecy. The intention is rather to picture characteristics of the church in all ages, and to give
messages of warning and encouragement to every local
church and to every individual member, during all the
coming years, until the return of Christ.

The vision which meets John, as he turns in the direc-
tion of the Voice, is that of "one like unto a son of man,"
standing in the midst of seven golden candlesticks. The

candlestick, or more exactly the lamp stand, was not for the support of candles made of wax or some similar material; it held lamps in which oil was burned. Such a lamp stand was an accepted Old Testament symbol of the people of God, filled with his Spirit, and giving to a world of darkness the light of divine truth and life. So here the "seven golden candlesticks" represent the church of Christ, which is divinely appointed to be the light of the world.

To this church seven letters are to be sent. However, the vision is centered first upon the Lord, whose message the letters will convey. He is presented in an aspect of priestly dignity and kingly majesty. He stands among the churches ready to reprove and to protect, to punish and to reward. He is described by John as "clothed with a garment down to the foot, and girt about at the breasts with a golden girdle. And his head and his hair were white as white wool, white as snow; and his eyes were as a flame of fire, and his feet like unto burnished brass, as if it had been refined in a furnace; and his voice as the voice of many waters. And he had in his right hand seven stars: and out of his mouth proceeded a sharp two-edged sword: and his countenance was as the sun shineth in his strength."

This is Oriental imagery. The picture is not for the crayon or the brush. The mind must rest not on the symbol but on that which the symbol represents. One is not to paint a mental picture of the robe, high-girdled and reaching to the ground, but to think of One who occupies a place of high rank and royal power. The white hair, like sunlight gleaming on snow, pictures divine purity. The eyes flashing with fire picture divine knowledge piercing to the innermost secrets of the heart. The feet of burnished brass represent the ability to tread down all opposition. The Voice was, to John, like the sound of the surf roaring on the shore of his rocky isle, a symbol of irresistible power. The right hand holding the seven stars shows the angels of the churches to be under the absolute control of Christ and under his protecting care. The sharp sword proceeding out of his mouth is an image of his word of judgment which can punish and destroy, which none can resist or escape. The countenance like the unclouded sun symbolizes the heavenly glory and majesty of Him upon whom, with unveiled face, none could dare to gaze. Thus the vision is not of One who is all tenderness and mercy, but of One who also is ready to punish, to judge, and to destroy. No wonder that at such a vision of Christ, John "fell at his feet as one dead"! Every vision of divine purity and majesty and power inspires awe and reverence and holy fear. Yet Christ is full of compassion and love. For all who are penitent and humble there is not only pardon but there are words of cheer and there is a task assigned.

"And he laid his right hand upon me, saying, Fear not." This is a touch of comfort and a commission to a great service. It is intended to give courage, not to John alone, but to the whole church, to whom, through John, a message is being sent. This church is to be associated with Christ in a great conflict, yet this church need not fear. Christ is eternal in his divine being: "I am the first and the last, and the Living one." He has accomplished a great redeeming work: "I was dead, and behold, I am alive for evermore." He has authority over life and death, and is yet to be victorious over all foes: "I have the keys of death and of Hades."

It is in view of such divine power, and as the agent of such a divine Person, that John is commissioned to compose his prophecy: "Write therefore the things which thou sawest, and the things which are, and the things which shall come to pass hereafter." These three phrases are understood to contain a rough outline of the Revelation: "The things which thou sawest," denoting the first chapter; "the things which are," comprising the second and third chapters; and "the things which shall come to pass hereafter," including the rest of the book. There are serious objections to this popular view. The first division, and indeed the second, would be disproportionately brief. Furthermore, portions of the third division refer to the birth of Christ and to other events of the past and present. It is more probable that "the things which thou sawest" is anticipatory of all the visions, and the phrases mean, "Write what thou hast seen both of the present and of the future." The whole prophecy is then defined as "the mystery of the seven stars . . . and the seven golden candlesticks." A "mystery" is, in New Testament usage, truth or reality divinely revealed. Thus John is to write a divine revelation concerning the Christian church. His whole prophecy is to relate to its development, its deliverance, its ultimate glory.

Such is the interpretation given by the King James Version and also by the American Standard Version of the Bible. There are some translators, however, who prefer to begin a new sentence with the words, "The mystery of the seven stars." The meaning, then, of "the mystery of the seven stars . . . and the seven golden candlesticks" is this: "The seven stars are the angels of the seven churches: and the seven candlesticks are seven churches."

There is great difficulty in determining what is meant by "the angels of the seven churches." The phrase commonly is supposed to designate the "pastors" or "bishops" of the individual churches. However, it is quite uncertain that such officers, as distinct from the governing board of "presbyters" or "bishops," existed in the local churches; and furthermore, the word "angel" is used some sixty times in this book and never elsewhere to denote a human being. "Guardian angels" have been suggested; but is there proof that such have been appointed for each church, and, if so, how can these have been open to the rebukes and reproofs addressed to them in the seven letters which follow?

Therefore many conclude that the "angel" in each case refers to "the prevailing spirit" of the church; it is a personification of the character and temper and conduct of the church. It expresses the idea that each church, with its many individual members, constitutes a unity. So, too, the figure seven indicates that the several local churches are actually one. The vision, therefore, which introduces the letters to the seven churches vividly portrays the presence of the living Christ with his church in all places and through all the ages. As his glorious Presence is realized, the result cannot fail to be more of purity and more of loyalty, more too of steadfastness and of heroic endurance, amidst all the scenes of tribulation and disaster which the Apocalypse reveals.

2. TO THE CHURCH IN EPHESUS   Ch. 2:1-7

1 To the angel of the church in Ephesus write:

These things saith he that holdeth the seven stars in his right hand, he that walketh in the midst of the seven golden candlesticks: 2 I know thy works, and thy toil and patience, and that thou canst not bear evil men, and didst try them that call themselves apostles, and they are not, and didst find them false; 3 and thou hast patience and didst bear for my name's sake, and hast not grown weary. 4 But I have this against thee, that thou didst leave thy first love. 5 Remember therefore whence thou art fallen, and repent and do the first works; or else I come to thee, and will move thy candlestick out of its place, except thou repent. 6 But this thou hast, that thou hatest the works of the Nicolaitans, which I also hate. 7 He that hath an ear, let him hear what the Spirit saith to the churches. To him that overcometh, to him will I give to eat of the tree of life, which is in the Paradise of God.

The letters to the seven churches are composed in accordance with the most careful and exact literary scheme. Each one consists of the same seven parts: a superscription to the church addressed; a description of the divine Author; an account of the spiritual condition of the church; an appropriate message of praise or censure; exhortations in view of the special need; a promise to "him that overcometh"; and a call to attention: "He that hath an ear, let him hear what the Spirit saith to the churches." The only apparent interruption in this symmetry is in the case of this call to attention. In each of the first three letters it precedes the promise to the overcomer; in the last four letters it follows this promise. However, this is in accordance with a larger symmetry, noticeable elsewhere, whereby the number seven is divided into its two parts of three and four, or four and three.

Together with this uniformity in the literary scheme, there is a striking contrast in the actual content of each letter. With keen insight the prophet penetrates into the moral and religious life of each church and paints a picture which is absolutely distinct. While all seven churches combined furnish the characteristics to be noted in the universal church, which are noted for that reason, yet undoubtedly there was in mind, in each case, an actual church then existing in the province of Asia and possessing the features set forth in the letter to that particular church.

Furthermore, there was some relation between the character of each church and the city in which it was located. This fact, however, is often exaggerated. The moral condition of the church and the spiritual message of the letter are hidden by some interpreters beneath a mass of archaeological and historic details. It does add, however, an atmosphere of reality when it is remembered that these letters were addressed to actual churches in cities which once played their part in the history of the world.

It is natural that the first church to be addressed is the church in Ephesus. This city was the capital of the province and its chief commercial and religious center, and was called "The Light of Asia." It was the terminus of the great system of Roman roads which constituted the trade route westward from the Euphrates Valley. It was celebrated for its temple of Diana (Artemis), one of the Seven

Wonders of the World, and was a hotbed of every false religious cult and superstition. Here Paul had founded a church and, during a protracted stay of more than two years, had projected a movement by which the whole province was evangelized. Here, too, if the tradition is accepted, John had labored, and thither he returned from exile to continue the work of his declining years. It might be expected that the first message would be sent to the church in this principal city, the church nearest to the apostle's own heart.

The actual Author, however, is not John but the living Christ, who is described in a phrase taken from the vision of ch. 1: "These things saith he that holdeth the seven stars in his right hand, he that walketh in the midst of the seven golden candlesticks." By some such phrase each letter is linked to the vision of the divine Lord. Here there is a slight added emphasis. "Holdeth" is a stronger word than "had," which was used in recording the vision. Here Christ not only stands but "walketh" amidst the candlesticks, and he is not only near to the one church addressed; he is moving about among all the churches, ready to reprove, to rescue, and to control.

The church in Ephesus is warmly praised for its "toil and patience," for its hatred of evil men, and for its refusal to accept false teachers who came in the guise of apostles. The steadfastness of the church is further emphasized. For the sake of Christ, for his "name's sake," the church has borne the labor of opposing those who would have corrupted the gospel, and has "not grown weary" of the task. Loyalty to the truth, orthodoxy of belief, was the outstanding virtue of the Ephesian church.

However, the church had fallen into the temptation to which defenders of the faith are peculiarly exposed, namely, that of censoriousness, suspicion, bitterness, factiousness. The rebuke is severe: "But I have this against thee, that thou didst leave thy first love." This love was love for Christ and love for fellow Christians. The two are inseparable. The very endeavor to distinguish between them, and to claim that one may possess the former when lacking the latter, is an intimation of fault. Brotherly love is always a test and an expression of genuine faith. Real devotion to Christ and his truth will manifest itself in charity. Zeal for pure doctrine easily degenerates into hatred for those who differ in their beliefs. It is possible for a church to be sound in doctrine and patient under persecution, and yet to be guilty of having left the love which it once displayed.

Such a condition is serious. Not to love is not to live. The call to repentance is solemn and insistent: "Remember therefore whence thou art fallen, and repent and do the first works; or else I come to thee, and will move thy candlestick out of its place, except thou repent." The first necessity is to realize that there has been a lapse of devotion; penitence must be shown and recovery made possible, not by empty protestation or display of emotion, but by deeds of love: "Repent and do the first works." Under no other condition can the church continue to exist.

While failing in love, the church in Ephesus was not guilty of the fault of believing that doctrine may be divorced from duty, that creed may be separated from character, that an intellectual acceptance of truth is more important than moral conduct. Into such an error the church had not fallen: "But this thou hast, that thou hatest the works of the Nicolaitans, which I also hate."

The exact origin of this sect and the character of its beliefs are open to dispute; but there seems to be agreement as to the fact that it allowed and practiced positive immorality on the ground of spiritual liberty. Such false ideas of freedom from the law, of the right to "continue in sin, that grace may abound," early invaded the Christian church. Toward such an attitude of mind the believers in Ephesus had shown only detestation and hate.

To this church a final promise is addressed. But it is introduced by a formula which widens the application of the promise to all churches at all times: "He that hath an ear, let him hear what the Spirit saith to the churches. To him that overcometh, to him will I give to eat of the tree of life, which is in the Paradise of God."

The Christian life will always be a conflict. There ever will be foes to endanger soundness of doctrine, charity of judgment, purity of conduct. Yet to each soldier of the cross there is this word of encouragement. Let him by patient endurance and loyal obedience reject all false beliefs and resist all allurements to sin, and he will receive, as his reward, life in all its fullness. He will partake of a blessed immortality in a "Paradise Regained." He will "eat of the tree of life" in the garden of God.

3. To the Church in Smyrna Ch. 2:8-11

8 And to the angel of the church in Smyrna write:

These things saith the first and the last, who was dead, and lived again: 9 I know thy tribulation, and thy poverty (but thou art rich), and the blasphemy of them that say they are Jews, and they are not, but are a synagogue of Satan. 10 Fear not the things which thou art about to suffer: behold, the devil is about to cast some of you into prison, that ye may be tried; and ye shall have tribulation ten days. Be thou faithful unto death, and I will give thee the crown of life. 11 He that hath an ear, let him hear what the Spirit saith to the churches. He that overcometh shall not be hurt of the second death.

Following the letter to the church in Ephesus, it is natural that the church in Smyrna should be addressed. The city lay only forty miles to the north of Ephesus and was second only to Ephesus in position and importance. Because of the charm of its location and the attractiveness of its appearance it was known as "The Beauty of Asia." It was wealthy, prosperous, dissolute, and famed as a center of emperor worship. Its large number of Jews were bitter opponents of Christianity. The church in such a city might be exposed naturally to opposition and persecution. Such, indeed, was the case, and the church of Smyrna is known as the "suffering church."

Thus it is fitting that the message is sent as from Him who is "the first and the last, who was dead, and lived again." As in the case of the address which opens each letter, this is a reference to the vision of Christ (ch. 1). Yet the address is also in each instance appropriate to the particular church. So here, to the martyr church, comes a word of cheer from the Lord who has triumphed over death and the grave.

The living Christ assures the members of the suffering church that he is acquainted perfectly with their condition: "I know thy tribulation, and thy poverty (but thou art rich), and the blasphemy of them that say they are Jews, and they are not, but are a synagogue of Satan." Their "tribulation" is severe. It probably produced their "poverty," open assault being united with a spoiling of their goods. It was accompanied by vilification and slander. This form of "blasphemy" is attributed to Jews, who, however, were such in name only. In reality they were a group which was the instrument of Satan. Yet worse trials are to come: "The devil is about to cast some of you into prison, that ye may be tried; and ye shall have tribulation ten days." Tribulation will deepen into martyrdom: "Be thou faithful unto death." In the face of such tribulation, penury, slander, imprisonment, martyrdom, what is the encouragement offered to the church in Smyrna, and so to all believers who suffer because of their loyalty to Christ?

First of all is the assurance that Christ knows. In all their distress, and in spite of the mystery, they have the companionship of a living and sympathetic Savior: "I know thy tribulation."

Secondly, there is the assurance that their poverty is only seeming. It is not real. Those who belong to Christ possess the true riches. Theirs are spiritual treasures which no enemy ever can take away.

Then, too, there is comfort in knowing that the divine estimate reverses false claims of men. The real people of God are not those who are Jews by birth or by name. The church is the true heir of the promises. Israelites who blaspheme the name of Christ are mere emissaries of Satan. Also, there is the assurance that a definite limit is set to the suffering of these true Christians. It may seem long, but it will continue only "ten days."

However, the chief comfort is contained in the very words which indicate that more dreadful suffering is to come. The fact is not concealed. For some of these readers there is a certainty of death as martyrs. Yet this is the assurance of the risen Christ, who himself has conquered death: "Be thou faithful unto death, and I will give thee the crown of life." That crown of royalty, or that garland of victory, will consist of life eternal, life celestial, life immortal, in fellowship with the living Christ.

Thus the letter closes with the promise to everyone who stands steadfast, enduring hardship and tribulation even to the suffering of martyrdom: "He that overcometh shall not be hurt of the second death." He may suffer the death of the body, but not of the soul. The living Lord who sustains him in the hour of anguish will welcome him home. For him there is no doom, no "lake of fire" which is "the second death" (ch. 20:14). His name will be "found written in the book of life" (v. 15).

4. TO THE CHURCH IN PERGAMUM   Ch. 2:12-17

12 And to the angel of the church in Pergamum write: These things saith he that hath the sharp two-edged sword: 13 I know where thou dwellest, even where Satan's throne is; and thou holdest fast my name, and didst not deny my faith, even in the days of Antipas my witness, my faithful one, who was killed among you, where Satan dwelleth. 14 But I have a few things against thee, because thou hast there some that hold the teaching of Balaam, who taught Balak to cast a stumblingblock before the children of Israel, to eat things sacrificed to idols, and to commit fornication. 15 So hast thou also some that hold the teach-

ing of the Nicolaitans in like manner. 16 Repent there-
fore; or else I come to thee quickly, and I will make war
against them with the sword of my mouth. 17 He that
hath an ear, let him hear what the Spirit saith to the
churches. To him that overcometh, to him will I give of
the hidden manna, and I will give him a white stone, and
upon the stone a new name written, which no one knoweth
but he that receiveth it.

Like Ephesus and Smyrna in beauty and wealth, Pergamum was also a great religious center. It was a perfect
pantheon of pagan deities. Of special fame was the temple of Aesculapius, to which from all parts of the world
sufferers came in search of healing. Yet above all else
the city prided itself upon its leadership in the worship of
the Roman emperors; and it is probably for this reason the
declaration is made that in Pergamum "Satan's throne is."

However, even in Pergamum a church was established.
In such surroundings it was not easy to be loyal to Christ.
All the forces of evil would continually oppose. The
church was in need of encouragement. This was supplied
in part by the descriptive phrase which opens the letter:
"These things saith he that hath the sharp two-edged
sword." In referring to the vision of Christ which precedes the seven letters, it will be remembered that this
"sharp two-edged sword" proceeded out of his mouth (ch.
1:16). It was thus the symbol of his word, ready to
avenge all disobedience, and also able to fight against his
enemies and to destroy them.

There is the further encouragement that the Lord knows
the temptation by which the church is surrounded: "I
know where thou dwellest, even where Satan's throne is."
He also knows their loyalty to him. He sees that like the
Christian martyr Antipas they are willing to lay down their
lives for his name: "Thou holdest fast my name, and didst
not deny my faith, even in the days of Antipas my witness,
my faithful one, who was killed among you."

The church, however, was not free from fault. There

were some of its members who deserved the most severe discipline. They formed a small minority. <u>The church did not sympathize with these offenders, but it was indifferent to their presence and to their evil influence</u>: "But I have a few things against thee, because thou hast there some that hold the teachings of Balaam, who taught Balak to cast a stumblingblock before the children of Israel, to eat things sacrificed to idols, and to commit fornication." It is a fair question how far the words are to be taken literally. All complicity with idolatry was regarded rightfully as unfaithfulness to the Lord. Even professing Christians, while not guilty of actual moral impurity, might hold lax views as to idolatrous practices, and might defend the right to compromising intimacies with idolaters. Persons who held and taught such views, even though not guilty of the more flagrant faults which are named, might well be compared to <u>Balaam</u>. His disgraceful influence is easily recalled. <u>He feared God but worshiped gold.</u> Failing to curse Israel, and so forfeiting the reward offered by Balak, he gave the diabolical counsel by which Israel was led to sin and so to grievous loss. The offenders in the church at Pergamum are compared to this ancient magician and prophet and seducer.

Furthermore, these false teachers are apparently identified with the Nicolaitans. In any event, the fault is the same, namely, the theory that one can be a Christian and yet be free to follow the practices of the sinful and godless: "So hast thou also some that hold the teaching of the Nicolaitans in like manner."

Therefore, the warning is addressed not only to the few flagrant offenders but to the whole church, which is guilty of moral indifference and too great tolerance of evil. It has not agreed with the false teachers, but it has failed to expel them from its fellowship. The whole church accordingly is called to repentance, but only the offenders are threatened: "Repent therefore; or else I come to thee quickly, and I will make war against them with the sword of my mouth." What this divine visitation might involve one only can conjecture. Evidently it implied some infliction upon the guilty far more serious than the most severe censure which the church might have imposed.

To those who are victorious over all pagan seductions, to those who refuse to yield to the threats of the imperial cult, great blessings are promised, the exact nature of which it is difficult to ascertain: "To him that overcometh, to him will I give of the hidden manna, and I will give him a white stone, and upon the stone a new name written, which no one knoweth but he that receiveth it." The reward seems to consist in fuller communion with Christ and a more perfect knowledge of God. Balaam tempted Israel in the wilderness, but there God fed his people with bread from heaven. The one who resists the temptation of evil will enjoy a secret and deeper fellowship with the Bread of life. Furthermore, to him will be given a new revelation of God, "a white stone" on which there will be "a new name written."

5. To the Church in Thyatira   Ch. 2:18-29

18 And to the angel of the church in Thyatira write:
These things saith the Son of God, who hath his eyes like a flame of fire, and his feet are like unto burnished brass: 19 I know thy works, and thy love and faith and ministry and patience, and that thy last works are more than the first. 20 But I have this against thee, that thou sufferest the woman Jezebel, who calleth herself a prophetess; and she teacheth and seduceth my servants to commit fornication, and to eat things sacrificed to idols. 21 And I gave her time that she should repent; and she willeth not to repent of her fornication. 22 Behold, I cast her into a bed, and them that commit adultery with her into great tribulation, except they repent of her works. 23 And I will kill her children with death; and all the churches shall know that I am he that searcheth the reins and hearts: and I will give unto each one of you according to your works. 24 But to you I say, to the rest that are in Thyatira, as many as

have not this teaching, who know not the deep things of Satan, as they are wont to say; I cast upon you none other burden. 25 Nevertheless that which ye have, hold fast till I come. 26 And he that overcometh, and he that keepeth my works unto the end, to him will I give authority over the nations: 27 and he shall rule them with a rod of iron, as the vessels of the potter are broken to shivers; as I also have received of my Father: 28 and I will give him the morning star. 29 He that hath an ear, let him hear what the Spirit saith to the churches.

It has been noted that the longest of the seven letters is addressed to a church in the least important of the seven cities. Thyatira never became a metropolis; nor was it honored in the cultus of the emperors. However, it was a rich and busy commercial city and was known as a center for the manufacture and dyeing of woolen goods. This fact may call to mind Lydia, of Thyatira, who was a dealer in such goods. Her connection with the church in that city may have been a matter of importance at an earlier date. The letter to the church in Thyatira begins the second group of messages to the churches of Asia. In the first group, the church of Ephesus was characterized by loyalty to Christ which was lacking in love. In the church of Smyrna loyalty was tested by fire. In the church of Pergamum the loyalty was lacking in moral passion. Yet all three churches were true to the faith, and had not yielded to the assaults of evil.

In the case of the church of Thyatira, as of the churches in Sardis and Laodicea, the situation was far more serious. Here not merely a small minority was indifferent, but large numbers had actually yielded to the demoralizing influences of false teaching. Possibly for this reason Christ characterizes himself in the address of the letter as "the Son of God, who hath his eyes like a flame of fire, and his feet are like unto burnished brass." Thus he is able to penetrate into the secrets of all hearts, and he has power to punish and subdue.

Our Lord begins with words of praise. He commends the church not only for its charity and faith and helpful service and constant steadfastness, but for an actual increase in these virtues, for a marked growth in spiritual life and attainment: "I know thy works, and thy love and faith and ministry and patience, and that thy last works are more than the first."

However, there is occasion for severe rebuke: "But I have this against thee, that thou sufferest the woman Jezebel." This one sentence summarizes the serious offense. The church was tolerating such a woman, was showing something of sympathy for her, and was allowing her and her followers to remain in its midst unrebuked and unopposed. The character of this woman is indicated by the name "Jezebel." That same calls to mind the imperious, indomitable Phoenician princess who, centuries before, had married Ahab, king of Israel. She was a fanatical worshiper of Baal, and had seduced the nation from loyalty to Jehovah to the practice of the impure rites of the heathen cult.

A woman of like character was corrupting the church at Thyatira. She is further described as one "who calleth herself a prophetess." That is, she was claiming inspiration and was pretending to disclose divine mysteries. Her influence, however, was most pernicious: "She teacheth and seduceth my servants to commit fornication, and to eat things sacrificed to idols."

Her conduct was not only flagrantly immoral; it was obstinate and defiant. It abused the divine patience and despised the divine warnings: "I gave her time that she should repent; and she willeth not to repent of her fornication."

The charge need not be interpreted with absolute literalness. Evidently this corrupt and corrupting leader was teaching, as profound mysteries, doctrines which were destructive of Christian faith and subversive of morality. She was a type of the false teachers who have ever threatened

the life of the church by boasted visions and perverted doctrines, maintaining that high spiritual experience can be
combined with degrading fleshly indulgence. So, too,
there is something figurative but terrible in the threatened
punishment: "Behold, I cast her into a bed, and them that
commit adultery with her into great tribulation. . . . And
I will kill her children with death." Just what is meant by
this "bed" of suffering, and what form of "tribulation" and
"death" are to be visited upon this woman and her accom-
plices and her victims, one cannot conjecture. However,
the visitation is to be so manifest and so dread as to be a
witness to "all the churches" that Christ searches the hearts
and rewards his followers according to their works.

Yet not the whole church at Thyatira has been deceived
by this Jezebel. To those who have not been misled a
message of gracious encouragement and promise is addressed. They have not accepted "this teaching"; they
have not been shown "the deep things of Satan" of which
the followers of Jezebel boast. Therefore upon them is
placed "none other burden" than the enmity and opposition of the apostate leaders. Until the appearing of Christ
they must "hold fast" the faith and the purity so far maintained. To them, if victorious in their conflict against
compromising seduction, there is the promise of sharing in
the triumph and the reign of Christ, even in the conquest
of all enemies and the universal rule which he has "received" from his Father.

They are promised even Christ himself. They will share
a fuller knowledge of his glory. They will partake of his
holiness, his virtues, his brightness: "I will give him the
morning star." Such a gift is assured to each one who in
days of testing is true to Christ and to the purity and holiness which loyalty to him demands.

6. To the Church in Sardis   Ch. 3:1-6

1 And to the angel of the church in Sardis write:
These things saith he that hath the seven Spirits of God,

and the seven stars: I know thy works, that thou hast a name that thou livest, and thou art dead. 2 Be thou watchful, and establish the things that remain, which were ready to die: for I have found no works of thine perfected before my God. 3 Remember therefore how thou hast received and didst hear; and keep it, and repent. If therefore thou shalt not watch, I will come as a thief, and thou shalt not know what hour I will come upon thee. 4 But thou hast a few names in Sardis that did not defile their garments: and they shall walk with me in white; for they are worthy. 5 He that overcometh shall thus be arrayed in white garments; and I will in no wise blot his name out of the book of life, and I will confess his name before my Father, and before his angels. 6 He that hath an ear, let him hear what the Spirit saith to the churches.

The city of Sardis lay some thirty miles southeast of Thyatira. It was the ancient capital of Lydia. While it had lost most of its former glory, it was still known for its wealth, and also for its wickedness. The church in Sardis was in a sad state of spiritual decline.

In addressing the church, the Author fittingly describes himself as "he that hath the seven Spirits of God," that is, as the Christ, the anointed One, upon whom the divine Spirit abides in all the perfection of his operation and power. He holds, he controls, "the seven stars"—either the ministers of the churches or the very churches themselves. He is even able and ready to impart spiritual life; and such life was lacking in the church now addressed: "I know thy works, that thou hast a name that thou livest, and thou art dead." The church has a reputation for activity. Probably its services are well attended and properly conducted. It may have committees and anniversaries and rallies. It may number among its members prominent social leaders. Yet it is dead. There are two particular proofs. First, it is accomplishing nothing in the spiritual realm: souls are not being saved; saints are not being strengthened; help is not being rendered to those in need; its services are formal, lifeless, meaningless: "I have found no works of thine perfected before my God." Secondly, the lives of the church members are stained by sin. Only a few "did not defile their garments."

To such a church Christ makes his gracious and patient appeal: "Be thou watchful, and establish the things that remain, which were ready to die." The admonition to be "watchful" may have been suggested by the fact that twice in its history the citadel of Sardis fell into the hands of the enemy because of a lack of vigilance on the part of the defenders—once in the days of Croesus, 549 B.C., and again when captured by Antiochus the Great, in 218 B.C. The church accordingly is exhorted to watch, but also to "establish the things that remain." There is some continuing spiritual consciousness to which an appeal could be made. There are some elements of life to be cultivated. Whatever of love or faith or piety remains must be established. Even the existing forms of worship may be given vitality. The empty ceremonies need not be discarded, but may be used to express emotions and sentiments which are real.

To stimulate the church to action, an appeal is made to the memory of better days, and to the joy and eagerness with which the gospel was first welcomed: "Remember therefore how thou hast received and didst hear; and keep it, and repent"; and the warning is added: "If therefore thou shalt not watch, I will come as a thief, and thou shalt not know what hour I will come upon thee." The coming of Christ is a blessed hope, yet to those who are unprepared it may be an event of terror and surprise.

The situation in the church is evidently serious; more so, indeed, than in the church of Thyatira. However, not all the members have been guilty of spiritual deadness, and not all have been stained by heathen impurities: "But thou hast a few names in Sardis that did not defile their garments." To such the Master gives his promise: "They shall walk with me in white; for they are worthy."

This word of encouragement is now repeated with the

promise to the overcomer which closes this letter, as in some form it ends each of the seven letters: "He that overcometh shall thus be arrayed in white garments." The one who overcomes is the one who conquers his spiritual lethargy, who recalls his early devotion to Christ, who repents of his sins, and, particularly, who continues to keep his garments "unspotted from the world." He who has walked in the white robes of purity will hereafter walk in the white robes of victory, of gladness, and of glory. "And I will in no wise blot his name out of the book of life." This is significantly added, for those who have fought to maintain their spiritual life are promised thus an endless felicity in the city of God. Their names "are written in heaven." Furthermore, these names found in "the book of life" will be acknowledged before the "Father, and before his angels." This blessed promise is not for the members of the church at Sardis alone, but for all the faithful, in the ages of trial and spiritual deadness to come; for the familiar formula is added: "He that hath an ear, let him hear what the Spirit saith to the churches."

7. TO THE CHURCH IN PHILADELPHIA
Ch. 3:7-13

7 And to the angel of the church in Philadelphia write: These things saith he that is holy, he that is true, he that hath the key of David, he that openeth and none shall shut, and that shutteth and none openeth: 8 I know thy works (behold, I have set before thee a door opened, which none can shut), that thou hast a little power, and didst keep my word, and didst not deny my name. 9 Behold, I give of the synagogue of Satan, of them that say they are Jews, and they are not, but do lie; behold, I will make them to come and worship before thy feet, and to know that I have loved thee. 10 Because thou didst keep the word of my patience, I also will keep thee from the hour of trial, that hour which is to come upon the whole world, to try them that dwell upon the earth. 11 I come quickly: hold fast that which

*thou hast, that no one take thy crown. 12 He that over-
cometh, I will make him a pillar in the temple of my God,
and he shall go out thence no more: and I will write upon
him the name of my God, and the name of the city of my
God, the new Jerusalem, which cometh down out of heaven
from my God, and mine own new name. 13 He that hath
an ear, let him hear what the Spirit saith to the churches.*

The Philadelphian church was the church of privilege,
the church of the "open door." It was not large in numbers. The city in which it was located was unimportant
and had suffered greatly from earthquakes. However, the
city was on the direct route to the highlands of central
Asia Minor, and the church of Philadelphia thus had unusual opportunities of evangelizing the inner provinces.
Of such opportunities the church seems to have taken full
advantage, and the letter to this church is an encouragement to enter every open door of service and thus to secure an abiding influence for good.

The Author describes himself as "he that is holy, he
that is true." "The Holy One" is a term which in the Old
Testament is applied to deity. Here the word "holy" denotes the divine sanctity of Christ as separated from all
limitations and imperfections. He is also "true," as fulfilling the divine ideal and also as constant to his plighted
word.

Further, it is "he that hath the key of David, he that
openeth and none shall shut, and that shutteth and none
openeth." The key was a symbol of authority and rule.
All the promises made to the royal house of David are
fulfilled in the exaltation of Christ, who has been set over
the house of God and who has "all authority . . . in
heaven and on earth." No introduction could be more
fitting in a letter which is to deal with the doors of opportunity, which, when Christ opens them, none can close.

To this church, as to the church of Smyrna, there is
given no word of criticism or rebuke. The formula, "I
know thy works," is followed by no word of reproof but

by a parenthesis in which is set forth the peculiar privilege
of the church: "Behold, I have set before thee a door
opened, which none can shut." The advantageous situation of Philadelphia has been used by the church for a
wide proclamation of the gospel, and as a reward the opportunity for usefulness is to be continued.

The fidelity and missionary zeal are enhanced by the
fact that the church has but little social influence and is
small in membership. It has but "little power." Moreover, its testimony is opposed. The possibility of service
has not precluded the necessity for sacrifice and suffering.
Such is implied by the words of Christ: "Thou . . . didst
keep my word, and didst not deny my name."

The source of opposition is indicated by the words
which follow. It has not been caused by pagan persecution from without or from doctrinal corruption within the
church, but evidently from the enmity of unbelieving Jews.
These do not deserve the name of Jews. While persecuting the church they should be regarded as "the synagogue
of Satan." They "say they are Jews, and they are not, but
do lie." However, they will yet recognize the church as
the true "Israel of God" and pay homage to the followers
of Christ: "I will make them to come and worship before
thy feet, and to know that I have loved thee."

More severe trials are to come, but in these the church
will be kept by the power of Christ. This promise is made
in view of the fidelity shown by the church: "Because thou
didst keep the word of my patience." This phrase seems
to mean, "The preaching of that steadfast endurance with
which amid present hardships Christ is to be served." It
denotes loyal patience in suffering as well as courage in
confessing Christ.

"I also will keep thee from the hour of trial, that hour
which is to come upon the whole world, to try them that
dwell upon the earth." The "hour of trial" refers to the
times of trouble and disaster which precede the return of
Christ. In the foreshortened view of the prophet these

trials are near at hand and hardly distinguished from the persecutions which Christians already are enduring. In this hour of trial the church at Philadelphia will be safe. It is not easy to determine whether the words, "I also will keep thee from the hour," as used by John, mean safe emergence from the trial or entire escape from it. If the latter is the true interpretation of the words, the promise must refer to the fact that at the appearance of Christ the church will be delivered from the "bowls" of wrath, and the devastating judgments which are predicted by the prophet as yet to be visited upon an impenitent world.

This return of Christ is regarded as near: "I come quickly." It is an event which may occur in any generation. Then the deliverance of the church will be complete. Such a hope should be an incentive to loyal effort: "Hold fast that which thou hast, that no one take thy crown." Each church has its own responsibility; each individual has his own task and his own talents. Each one must be faithful. Otherwise the opportunity will be lost and the privilege seized by one more alert; and the prize for loyalty may be forfeited and another may win the crown.

The promise to the overcomer, as in each of the seven letters, is addressed to the individual members of the church. It is an assurance of permanent incorporation in the temple of God, the temple which is "built upon the foundation of the apostles and prophets, Christ Jesus himself being the chief corner stone": "He that overcometh, I will make him a pillar in the temple of my God, and he shall go out thence no more." Furthermore, each such pillar is to be inscribed with three new names. These are signs and seals of immortal blessedness. "I will write upon him the name of my God," indicating a complete consecration to the service of God; "and the name of the city of my God, the new Jerusalem, which cometh down out of heaven from my God," denoting an inalienable citizenship in the celestial city; "and mine own new name," a symbol of the fuller knowledge of Christ which will be revealed at his coming, when "we shall see him even as he is."

Such is the reward of each one who overcomes the temptation to faint and to prove false in the face of opposition and persecution; who, against all obstacles, continues faithfully to witness for Christ and to the power of his name.

8. TO THE CHURCH IN LAODICEA   Ch. 3:14-22

14 And to the angel of the church in Laodicea write:

These things saith the Amen, the faithful and true witness, the beginning of the creation of God: 15 I know thy works, that thou art neither cold nor hot: I would thou wert cold or hot. 16 So because thou art lukewarm, and neither hot nor cold, I will spew thee out of my mouth. 17 Because thou sayest, I am rich, and have gotten riches, and have need of nothing; and knowest not that thou art the wretched one and miserable and poor and blind and naked: 18 I counsel thee to buy of me gold refined by fire, that thou mayest become rich; and white garments, that thou mayest clothe thyself, and that the shame of thy nakedness be not made manifest; and eyesalve to anoint thine eyes, that thou mayest see. 19 As many as I love, I reprove and chasten: be zealous therefore, and repent. 20 Behold, I stand at the door and knock: if any man hear my voice and open the door, I will come in to him, and will sup with him, and he with me. 21 He that overcometh, I will give to him to sit down with me in my throne, as I also overcame, and sat down with my Father in his throne. 22 He that hath an ear, let him hear what the Spirit saith to the churches.

The letter to the church in Philadelphia contains no reproof. It is followed by the letter to the church in Laodicea, which contains no praise. The church was self-satisfied and unconscious of its need, a fact the more pitiful because the condition was actually so deplorable. The spiritual decline and apparent apostasy of the church may have been due in part to the material wealth of its members, to the luxury with which they were surrounded, and to the temptation to worldliness by which they were assailed. Laodicea was one of three neighboring cities in the Lycos Valley which are mentioned in the writings of Paul, the other two being Colossae and Hierapolis. It was a city of considerable wealth and commercial importance, and in connection with this letter it is interesting to note that two of its chief articles of trade were woolen cloth and eyesalve. Furthermore, the hot springs of Hierapolis, across the river Lycos, send forth water which, as it flows, soon becomes lukewarm and intolerable to the taste. The independence of the city was shown in its rejection of imperial help after the earthquake of A.D. 60. Evidently the church of Laodicea showed the same spirit of self-sufficiency as did the city, and so came to offer an illustration of proud complacency accompanying a low and indifferent spiritual life.

In addressing the church Christ calls himself "the Amen," the positive divine affirmation, whose promise is certain to be fulfilled; "the faithful and true witness," whose counsel is authoritative and should be laid to heart; "the beginning of the creation of God"—not a part of the creation, but "the uncreated principle of creation from whom it took its origin." "The Amen," the head of creation, bears his witness to the condition of this church and the very solemnity of his title prepares the way for the severity of the following rebuke: "I know thy works, that thou art neither cold nor hot: I would thou were cold or hot. So because thou art lukewarm, and neither hot nor cold, I will spew thee out of my mouth."

Tepid religion is nauseating. One who has made no profession of faith and is conscious of his utter lack of moral life and spiritual condition is in a far more hopeful condition than one who thinks himself to be a Christian and yet has no real spiritual life and is oblivious to his desperate need. So Christ looked with loathing on the

Pharisees of his day, who regarded themselves as religious paragons while their hearts were full of impurity and sin. For the publicans and sinners Christ had far more hope than for these proud hypocrites.

Yet the lukewarm church in Laodicea is serenely unconscious of its condition and absolutely unconcerned: "Thou sayest, I am rich, and have gotten riches, and have need of nothing." The church prides itself on its condition, which it ascribes to its own skill and effort. It is lukewarm and indifferent because of its self-deception and conceit. It is ignorant of its own state: "And knowest not that thou art the wretched one and miserable and poor and blind and naked," like a blind beggar barely clad. Such in reality is this rich and self-complacent church.

To such a church, Christ gives his solemn admonition: "I counsel thee to buy of me gold refined by fire," that is, a vital faith, purified and enriched by testing and by victory; "and white garments," the real clothing of the soul, consisting of righteous deeds and holy activities; "and eyesalve to anoint thine eyes"—not the eye powder of your local physicians, but "the anointing of the Spirit, whereby you will perceive your desperate need and behold the boundless grace of Christ." These gifts can be bought at the cost of real moral effort and humble repentance and courageous faith.

These worlds of severe rebuke are spoken in true sympathy and love. In spite of its deplorable condition, Christ does not despair of his church. "As many as I love, I reprove and chasten," is the message of the Lord, whose heart yearns over his self-complacent and lukewarm church. "Be zealous therefore, and repent."

To this call to repentance Christ adds the most tender message found in any of his letters. It is the more notable because addressed to the least deserving Christians: "Behold, I stand at the door and knock: if any man hear my voice and open the door, I will come in to him, and will sup with him, and he with me." Such is the promise to every individual, even in a church like Laodicea. Christ may have been shut out, the church may seem devoid of spiritual life, but wherever one heart is open to receive him, there Christ will enter, and will abide in blessed fellowship. Let no one excuse himself because of his surroundings or because of the state of his fellow Christians. This is the assurance: "If any man hear my voice and open the door, I will come in to him, and will sup with him."

Nor is the promise only one of communion; it is also one of sovereignty: "He that overcometh, I will give to him to sit down with me in my throne, as I also overcame, and sat down with my Father in his throne." To win in the struggle against self-indulgence and self-confidence and self-satisfaction is to conquer self now, but it is a preparation for a share in the beneficent and perfect rule of the exalted Christ. With such great realities sounding in our hearing, there comes again the stirring appeal: "He that hath an ear, let him hear what the Spirit saith to the churches."

B. THE SEVEN SEALS Chs. 4:1 to 8:1

1. INTRODUCTORY VISION: CHRIST IN THE PLACE OF POWER Chs. 4; 5

1 After these things I saw, and behold, a door opened in heaven, and the first voice that I heard, a voice as of a trumpet speaking with me, one saying, Come up hither, and I will show thee the things which must come to pass hereafter. 2 Straightway I was in the Spirit: and behold, there was a throne set in heaven, and one sitting upon the throne; 3 and he that sat was to look upon like a jasper stone and a sardius: and there was a rainbow round about the throne, like an emerald to look upon. 4 And round about the throne were four and twenty thrones: and upon the thrones I saw four and twenty elders sitting, arrayed in white garments; and on their heads crowns of gold. 5 And out of the throne proceed lightnings and voices and thunders.

And there were *seven lamps of fire burning before the throne, which are the seven Spirits of God; 6 and before the throne, as it were a sea of glass like unto crystal; and in the midst of the throne, and round about the throne, four living creatures full of eyes before and behind. 7 And the first creature was like a lion, and the second creature like a calf, and the third creature had a face as of a man, and the fourth creature was like a flying eagle. 8 And the four living creatures, having each one of them six wings, are full of eyes round about and within: and they have no rest day and night, saying,*

Holy, holy, holy, is the Lord God, the Almighty, who was and who is and who is to come.

9 *And when the living creatures shall give glory and honor and thanks to him that sitteth on the throne, to him that liveth for ever and ever, 10 the four and twenty elders shall fall down before him that sitteth on the throne, and shall worship him that liveth for ever and ever, and shall cast their crowns before the throne, saying,*

11 Worthy art thou, our Lord and our God, to receive the glory and the honor and the power: for thou didst create all things, and because of thy will they were, and were created.

5:1 And I saw in the right hand of him that sat on the throne a book written within and on the back, close sealed with seven seals. 2 And I saw a strong angel proclaiming with a great voice, Who is worthy to open the book, and to loose the seals thereof? 3 And no one in heaven, or on the earth, or under the earth, was able to open the book, or to look thereon. 4 And I wept much, because no one was found worthy to open the book, or to look thereon: 5 and one of the elders saith unto me, Weep not; behold, the Lion that is of the tribe of Judah, the Root of David, hath overcome to open the book and the seven seals thereof. 6 And I saw in the midst of the throne and of the four living creatures, and in the midst of the elders, a Lamb standing, as though it had been slain, having seven horns, and seven eyes, which are the seven Spirits of God, sent forth into all the earth. 7 And he came, and he taketh it out of the right hand of him that sat on the throne. 8 And when he had taken the book, the four living creatures and the

*four and twenty elders fell down before the Lamb, having
each one a harp, and golden bowls full of incense, which
are the prayers of the saints. 9 And they sing a new song,
saying,*

> *Worthy art thou to take the book, and to open the
> seals thereof: for thou wast slain, and didst purchase
> unto God with thy blood men of every tribe, and
> tongue, and people, and nation, 10 and madest them
> to be unto our God a kingdom and priests; and they
> reign upon the earth.*

*11 And I saw, and I heard a voice of many angels round
about the throne and the living creatures and the elders;
and the number of them was ten thousand times ten thousand, and thousands of thousands; 12 saying with a great
voice,*

> *Worthy is the Lamb that hath been slain to receive
> the power, and riches, and wisdom, and might, and
> honor, and glory, and blessing.*

*13 And every created thing which is in the heaven, and on
the earth, and under the earth, and on the sea, and all
things that are in them, heard I saying,*

> *Unto him that sitteth on the throne, and unto the
> Lamb, be the blessing, and the honor, and the glory,
> and the dominion, for ever and ever.*

*14 And the four living creatures said, Amen. And the
elders fell down and worshipped.*

The letters to the seven churches were designed to prepare the followers of Christ for the trials to which they
would be subjected before the return of their Lord. The
members of the churches were warned against impurity of
doctrine and of life. They were exhorted to active service
and fervent love. They were strengthened by promises of
great blessings, should they overcome and prove steadfast
amid all the persecutions and convulsions which the future
held in store.

These events of testing and disaster are pictured first as
accompanying the successive opening of the seven seals of
the book of destiny. However, before the opening of

these seals there is recorded a preparatory vision, in which it is shown that this book is in the hands of Christ. He has "all authority . . . in heaven and on earth." He can overrule the events of history so as to insure the safety of the church and the final establishment of his perfected Kingdom. Thus to encourage the church in view of impending events there is given this vision of Christ in the place of power.

In this vision the Creator intrusts to the Redeemer a seven-sealed book. The scene is laid in the court of heaven. The prophet in ecstatic rapture beholds, through an open door, the God of Israel seated upon a throne and surrounded by angelic hosts. The description of the Deity is reverent and restrained. He is "to look upon like a jasper stone and a sardius." The jasper, unlike modern stones of that name, was "clear as crystal" (ch. 21:11). Its sparkling brightness may picture the holiness of God. The fiery-red sardius may be an emblem of his avenging wrath. There was "a rainbow round about the throne, like an emerald to look upon," possibly a symbol of never-failing mercy.

"Round about the throne" are "four and twenty elders." They are seated upon thrones. They are "arrayed in white garments." On their heads are "crowns of gold." These are the ideal representatives of the glorified people of God. They call to mind the twelve patriarchs of the Old Testament, and the twelve apostles of the New.

"Out of the throne proceed lightnings and voices and thunders," symbols of divine judgment. "And there were seven lamps of fire burning before the throne, which are the seven Spirits of God." Thus the Holy Spirit, in his manifold operations, searches all things and is active everywhere in his judgments and his purifying power.

"And before the throne, as it were a sea of glass like unto crystal." This adds splendor to the scene. Between the door through which the prophet gazes and the throne on which the Creator is seated stretches this gleaming pavement, which flashes back the light as sunbeams are reflected from the summer sea.

Closely associated with the throne, circling about it, are "four living creatures," which unite the features of the cherubim and the seraphim, and stand as the symbols of the renewed and redeemed creation. They represent the highest order of beings and are the agents of divine judgment, the leaders of universal praise. They reecho the song of the seraphim: "Holy, holy, holy, is the Lord God, the Almighty." They add the notes of praise: "Who was and who is and who is to come." The last note, "Is to come," points forward to the time when God will manifest himself anew, and creation will be glorified, perfected, complete.

To the praise sounded by the "four living creatures" the elders sing a responsive song. They fall down in adoration. They "cast their crowns before the throne." They glorify Him to whom all creatures owe their being. Because of his will, "they were, and were created"; that is, the whole universe existed in the divine will, even in the eternal past, but at the Creation it was manifested in the sphere of visible being.

However, the interest of the vision centers in "a book" which the prophet sees "in the right hand of him that sat on the throne." Strictly speaking, it is a scroll, rolled together. It is "written within and on the back." The content is complete. Nothing more can be written. It contains all the decrees of God, an outline of all events to the very end of the age. What these contents are, the following chapters will disclose. Of them the prophet is ignorant. He knows that they must be of supreme importance, for he hears "a strong angel proclaiming with a great voice, Who is worthy to open the book, and to loose the seals thereof?"

To the deep distress of the prophet, "no one in heaven, or on the earth, or under the earth, was able to open the book, or to look thereon." As he records his sorrow he writes, "And I wept much, because no one was found worthy to open the book, or to look thereon." Then, to his great relief, one of the elders advances with the word of comfort: "Weep not; behold, the Lion that is of the tribe of Judah," that is, the chief Son of the royal tribe, he "hath overcome to open the book and the seven seals thereof." The prophet turns to see the Lion, and to his surprise he sees "a Lamb standing, as though it had been slain." A lamb, unlike a lion, is a symbol of meekness; and this Lamb has been slain—"slaughtered," as the word means. It is a Lamb which has been sacrificed. One need not be told that this is "the Lamb of God, that taketh away the sin of the world." This Lamb has overcome. His very death was the means of his victory, and one of the fruits of his triumph is his right to open the seals of God's book of destiny, to unlock the mystery of God's decrees, to bring to their ultimate issue all events as they culminate in the perfected Kingdom of God: "The Lion that is of the tribe of Judah . . . hath overcome to open the book and the seven seals thereof." He was slain but has risen in power. He now appears "having seven horns," symbols of his irresistible might. He has "seven eyes, which are the seven Spirits of God," symbolic of his searching vision, from which nothing can be hid.

In virtue of his triumph over sin and death "he came, and he taketh [the book] . . . out of the right hand of him that sat on the throne." This was the reward of the Victor. This was the investiture of the King. This was the recognition of the right of Christ to rule, and to control the events of the ages to come. No wonder that now "the four living creatures and the four and twenty elders fell down before the Lamb. . . . And they sing a new song, saying,

"Worthy art thou to take the book, and to open the seals thereof: for thou wast slain, and didst purchase unto God with thy blood men of every tribe, and tongue, and people, and nation."

No wonder an innumerable company of angels round about the throne take up the great refrain: "Worthy is the Lamb that hath been slain"! No wonder that "every created thing which is in the heaven, and on the earth" unites in the great chorus:

"Unto him that sitteth on the throne, and unto the Lamb, be the blessing, and the honor, and the glory, and the dominion, for ever and ever"!

This is the very music of heaven; and as we look back over the praises contained in these two chapters we find that they comprise in substance two great oratorios: The Oratorio of Creation (ch. 4), and The Oratorio of Redemption (ch. 5). It will be remembered that an oratorio is a musical composition in which solos and choruses combine to the accompaniment of instruments. Here the voices of angels and the elders with their harps form immortal choirs, chanting celestial praise.

The arrangement of these musical numbers is most artistic. The worship of the Creator begins with a quartet, as the "four living creatures" sing the seraphs' song:

"Holy, holy, holy, is the Lord God, the Almighty, who was and who is and who is to come."

This is followed by the choir, consisting of the twenty-four elders, which continues the praise of the Creator.

"Worthy art thou, our Lord and our God, to receive the glory and the honor and the power: for thou didst create all things, and because of thy will they were, and were created."

Then are heard the solo voices:

"Who is worthy to open the book, and to loose the seals thereof?"

And the response:

> "The Lion that is of the tribe of Judah, the Root of David, hath overcome to open the book and the seven seals thereof."

Then, as the Lamb takes the book out of the hand of the Creator, there is heard the unison of the quartet and the choir of elders singing the new song, saying,

> "Worthy art thou to take the book, and to open the seals thereof: for thou wast slain, and didst purchase unto God with thy blood men of every tribe, and tongue, and people, and nation, and madest them to be unto our God a kingdom and priests; and they reign upon the earth."

Then there bursts forth the majestic chorus. Angels are singing. "Ten thousand times ten thousand, and thousands of thousands" swell the triumphant strain:

> "Worthy is the Lamb that hath been slain to receive the power, and riches, and wisdom, and might, and honor, and glory, and blessing."

Now, with thrilling crescendo, the climax and grand finale are reached. Not only the "four living creatures," the elders, and the angels unite, but "every created thing which is in the heaven, and on the earth, and under the earth, and on the sea, and all things that are in them" is heard praising both the Creator and the Redeemer:

> "Unto him that sitteth on the throne, and unto the Lamb, be the blessing, and the honor, and the glory, and the dominion, for ever and ever."

Then, as the tumult of universal praise dies away, there is heard the sound of a grand "Amen." It is from the lips of the "four living creatures." A breathless silence follows, and the elders fall down and worship.

Such is the music of heaven. Therefore, the church on

earth need not fear, no matter how "fraught with punishments the scroll" of human history may be. For the meaning of the music is this: The Creator has given to the Redeemer "all authority . . . in heaven and on earth" and those who follow him will never pass "beyond His love and care."

2. THE FIRST SIX SEALS Ch. 6

1 And I saw when the Lamb opened one of the seven seals, and I heard one of the four living creatures saying as with a voice of thunder, Come. 2 And I saw, and behold, a white horse, and he that sat thereon had a bow; and there was given unto him a crown: and he came forth conquering, and to conquer.

3 And when he opened the second seal, I heard the second living creature saying, Come. 4 And another horse came forth, a red horse: and to him that sat thereon it was given to take peace from the earth, and that they should slay one another: and there was given unto him a great sword.

5 And when he opened the third seal, I heard the third living creature saying, Come. And I saw, and behold, a black horse; and he that sat thereon had a balance in his hand. 6 And I heard as it were a voice in the midst of the four living creatures saying, A measure of wheat for a shilling, and three measures of barley for a shilling; and the oil and the wine hurt thou not.

7 And when he opened the fourth seal, I heard the voice of the fourth living creature saying, Come. 8 And I saw, and behold, a pale horse: and he that sat upon him, his name was Death; and Hades followed with him. And there was given unto them authority over the fourth part of the earth, to kill with sword, and with famine, and with death, and by the wild beasts of the earth.

9 And when he opened the fifth seal, I saw underneath the altar the souls of them that had been slain for the word of God, and for the testimony which they held: 10 and they cried with a great voice, saying, How long, O Master, the holy and true, dost thou not judge and avenge our blood

*on them that dwell on the earth?   11 And there was given
them to each one a white robe; and it was said unto them,
that they should rest yet for a little time, until their fellow-
servants also and their brethren, who should be killed even
as they were, should have fulfilled* their course.

*12 And I saw when he opened the sixth seal, and there
was a great earthquake; and the sun became black as sackcloth of hair, and the whole moon became as blood;   13
and the stars of the heaven fell unto the earth, as a fig tree
casteth her unripe figs when she is shaken of a great wind.
14 And the heaven was removed as a scroll when it is rolled
up; and every mountain and island were moved out of their
places.   15 And the kings of the earth, and the princes, and
the chief captains, and the rich, and the strong, and every
bondman and freeman, hid themselves in the caves and in
the rocks of the mountains;   16 and they say to the mountains and to the rocks, Fall on us, and hide us from the face
of him that sitteth on the throne, and from the wrath of the
Lamb: 17 for the great day of their wrath is come; and
who is able to stand?*

With the opening of the sealed book in the hand of the
Redeemer, the dramatic movement of the Apocalypse actually begins.   The preceding chapters have been introductory.   The seven letters have shown the character, the
temptations, and the rewards of the church.   The vision
of the glorified Christ has revealed the creative power and
redeeming purpose of God.   The chapters now beginning
will present pictures of the sufferings of the church, the
divine judgments upon its enemies, and the ultimate triumph of Christ.   The first great cycle of visions shows a
series of events which follow the successive opening of
the seven seals of the book of destiny.   In these visions the
seer sweeps the whole horizon of the future.   The events
he records are typical.   No specific incidents are to be
sought for in human history exactly corresponding to the
occurrences here depicted.   The visions of the opening
seals describe movements which will characterize the entire age, from the ascension of Christ until his return in

glory. These are visions of peace and war, of famine and death, of persecution for the church, and of the revolutions and judgments in which the age will end.

As the first seal is opened, the prophet hears "one of the four living creatures saying as with a voice of thunder, Come." As the seals are broken the contents of the book are not read but its records are translated into action. This action in the case of each of the first four seals is announced by one of the "four living creatures" who are the executors of the divine decrees and the agents of divine judgment. The summons, "Come," is not addressed to Christ or to John, but to one of four horsemen. In response to the first summons, the prophet sees the appearing of "a white horse, and he that sat thereon had a bow; and there was given unto him a crown: and he came forth conquering, and to conquer." This is a vision of a widespread peace. The horseman has been supposed by some to represent Christ. The difficulty in such an interpretation lies in the fact that Christ appears in heaven, opening the seals, and not as an actor in the scene which unfolds. Then again, Christ can hardly be regarded as correlative and to be grouped with war and famine and death.

Others suppose that the rider on the white horse represents "victorious war." The objection is that this interpretation would confuse the first two horsemen and would deprive either one of meaning, for beyond question the second rider represents war. It is true that these two are closely related, forming in one sense a single vision introduced by the phrase, "And I saw," which is repeated in the case, not of the second, but of the third and fourth horsemen. However, the first and second horsemen are strikingly contrasted. The first represents the periods of peace granted, in the providence of God, under the Roman Empire, and to be repeated at various times in the history of the world.

Peace, however, is never permanent in this present age. For, as John writes, "When he opened the second seal, I heard the second living creature saying, Come. And another horse came forth, a red horse [a bloodred horse]: and to him that sat thereon it was given to take [the] peace from the earth." This picture of war is made more lurid by the added phrases: "That they should slay one another" and "There was given unto him a great sword," the merciless instrument of slaughter.

Famine follows war. Therefore we read: "When he opened the third seal . . . I saw, and behold, a black horse; and he that sat thereon had a balance in his hand. And I heard as it were a voice in the midst of the four living creatures saying, A measure of wheat for a shilling, and three measures of barley for a shilling; and the oil and the wine hurt thou not." To measure food by weight, in a "balance," indicates scarcity. This is further indicated by almost famine prices. However, the picture is not one of actual starvation; and the olive orchards and vineyards are not destroyed.

The conditions under the fourth seal are more severe. The color of the fourth horse is "pale," or the livid color of a corpse; and the name of the rider is "Death"; and "Hades followed with him" as his inseparable companion. These dread comrades appear to execute the judgments of God upon the earth. They accomplish their task by the use of four familiar and fearful instruments: sword, famine, pestilence, and wild beasts. However, the ravages of destruction are limited and restrained: "There was given unto them authority over" only "the fourth part of the earth."

With the opening of the fifth seal, the scene shifts from earth to heaven; yet the vision implies the peril and the persecution of the church on earth, and the comfort and encouragement of this church is the very purpose of the prophecy. The seer beholds "underneath the altar the souls of them that had been slain for the word of God, and for the testimony which they held." These, then, are the souls of martyrs, who have sealed with their blood the testimony they have borne to the one living and true God and to their Savior, Jesus Christ. Their souls are described as "underneath the altar"; probably because in the ancient sacrifices the blood, which was the symbol of life, was poured out at the foot of the altar.

These martyrs are heard crying out for vengeance: "How long, O Master, the holy and true, dost thou not judge and avenge our blood on them that dwell on the earth?" This cry is not a request for personal revenge, but for the vindication of divine justice. The expression is figurative. As "the blood of Abel" cried for vengeance on Cain, so "the souls" of the martyrs, their lives poured out as innocent victims, call for judgment on those who caused their death. However, while awaiting such judgment, the condition of the martyrs is one of blessedness. They are in heaven, for by contrast reference is made to their enemies "on the earth." They are in fellowship with Christ, for to him they address their appeal. They already have received the symbols of victory, of joy, and of glory; for "there was given them to each one a white robe." They are at "rest," like all those "who die in the Lord."

Yet their blessedness is not complete. "It was said unto them, that they should rest yet for a little time, until their fellow-servants also and their brethren, who should be killed even as they were, should have fulfilled their course." This is a message of tragedy and of triumph. It indicates that the days of martyrdom are not done. A further time of testing awaits the church on earth. Then the Lord will come, justice will be vindicated, and the martyrs in heaven and their fellow servants on earth together will share the victory of the King.

The opening of the sixth seal is described in a paragraph of rare majesty and power. Yet there is nothing new or original in the colors with which the prophet paints the scene. He borrows phrases which were repeatedly employed by the Old Testament writers and by our Lord himself as he depicted the events which would mark the end of the age. It is these last events, indeed, which the opening of the sixth seal is understood to disclose. The first four seals cover the whole period of the present age. They sketch its general character of mingled evil and good. They predict no particular time of peace or war or pestilence or famine. However, exactly as foretold in the prophetic discourses of Christ, as the age draws to its close there is to be a "great tribulation," and then scenes of catastrophe, followed by the coming of the Lord.

Just what is denoted by the details of the picture it is difficult to determine. What is pictured by the earthquake and the darkened sun and moon and by the falling stars, by the opened heaven and the moving mountains and islands? Do they depict social and political revolutions and cosmic convulsions? These "signs" which Christ foretold, as preceding his return, he did not interpret, nor does the prophet here explain. However, he does clearly describe the terror of an impenitent world. He mentions all classes of society, bond and free, in their futile atempt to escape. They are not so much afraid of death as of the revealed presence of God and the righteous anger of Christ. They are heard to say to the mountains and to the rocks, "Fall on us, and hide us from the face of him that sitteth on the throne, and from the wrath of the Lamb: for the great day of their wrath is come: and who is able to stand?" The sting of a guilty conscience, the torment of remorse, the dread of meeting a holy God and the face of a rejected Savior—these give more terror to the human soul than all the tumult of crashing empires, the approach of death, the most startling portents of earth and sea and sky. The "day of wrath" draws near, but "now is the acceptable time; . . . now is the day of salvation."

3. Episode: The Sealed and the Saved   Ch. 7.

1 After this I saw four angels standing at the four corners of the earth, holding the four winds of the earth, that no wind should blow on the earth, or on the sea, or upon any tree. 2 And I saw another angel ascend from the sunrising, having the seal of the living God: and he cried with a great voice to the four angels to whom it was given to hurt the earth and the sea, 3 saying, Hurt not the earth, neither the sea, nor the trees, till we shall have sealed the servants of our God on their foreheads. 4 And I heard the number of them that were sealed, a hundred and forty and four thousand, sealed out of every tribe of the children of Israel:

5 Of the tribe of Judah were sealed twelve thousand;
    Of the tribe of Reuben twelve thousand;
    Of the tribe of Gad twelve thousand;
6 Of the tribe of Asher twelve thousand;
    Of the tribe of Naphtali twelve thousand;
    Of the tribe of Manasseh twelve thousand;
7 Of the tribe of Simeon twelve thousand;
    Of the tribe of Levi twelve thousand;
    Of the tribe of Issachar twelve thousand;
8 Of the tribe of Zebulun twelve thousand;
    Of the tribe of Joseph twelve thousand;
    Of the tribe of Benjamin were sealed twelve thousand.

9 After these things I saw, and behold, a great multitude, which no man could number, out of every nation and of all tribes and peoples and tongues, standing before the throne and before the Lamb, arrayed in white robes, and palms in their hands; 10 and they cry with a great voice, saying,

    Salvation unto our God who sitteth on the throne,
    and unto the Lamb.

11 And all the angels were standing round about the throne, and about the elders and the four living creatures; and they fell before the throne on their faces, and worshipped God, 12 saying,

    Amen: Blessing, and glory, and wisdom, and thanksgiving, and honor, and power, and might, be unto our God for ever and ever. Amen.

13 And one of the elders answered, saying unto me, These that are arrayed in the white robes, who are they, and whence came they? 14 And I say unto him, My lord, thou knowest. And he said to me, These are they that come out of the great tribulation, and they washed their robes, and made them white in the blood of the Lamb. 15 Therefore

*are they before the throne of God; and they serve him day
and night in his temple: and he that sitteth on the throne
shall spread his tabernacle over them. 16 They shall hunger no more, neither thirst any more; neither shall the sun
strike upon them, nor any heat: 17 for the Lamb that is
in the midst of the throne shall be their shepherd, and shall
guide them unto fountains of waters of life: and God shall
wipe away every tear from their eyes.*

The signs of the sixth seal prepare us for the end of the
age and the coming of Christ. We expect him to appear
through the opening skies. Yet there is a sudden interruption, an unexpected episode. Before the seventh seal is
opened an interlude is introduced, a twofold picture representing the sealing of "the servants of our God" on earth
and the glory of the saints in heaven. The picture is
sketched against the dark background of dread and disaster which the sixth seal has disclosed. It is given to encourage the people of God amidst the terrors which sur-
round them, to assure them of their safety on the dread
"day of wrath," and to point them forward to the coming
Christ and their heavenly fellowship with him.

These parenthetic pictures of the security and triumph
of the church form a striking contrast to the panic and fear
of the impenitent world. When the first scene opens, there
appear "four angels standing at the four corners of the
earth, holding the four winds of the earth," to whom it is
given "to hurt the earth and the sea." These angels are
the agents of divine judgment. The fact that they are
"four," at the "four corners of the earth," holding "the four
winds of the earth," indicates, as the figure "four" would
intimate, that the judgment about to fall is universal.
None can escape. However, the judgment cannot descend
until the safety of the people of God has been secured.
Until then, "no wind should blow on the earth, or on the
sea, or upon any tree."

Another angel now appears, ascended "from the sunrising," a beautiful symbol of hope and cheer and deliver-

ance. This angel "cried with a great voice . . . , Hurt
not the earth, neither the sea, nor the trees, till we shall
have sealed the servants of our God on their foreheads."

This sealing denotes preservation in the midst of judgment. The conception is borrowed from the prophecy of
Ezekiel. (Ch. 9.) There a "man . . . with a writer's
inkhorn" is seen in Jerusalem, who sets a mark on the
foreheads of those who are to escape impending massacre.
Here, in the vision of John, it is not a mere "mark" that
is described, but a divine "seal." It is the sign made by
the signet ring of the great King. It designates those who
belong to him. They are in safety, "having this seal, The
Lord knoweth them that are his." Possibly something
more is implied. Believers are "sealed with the Holy
Spirit . . . unto the redemption of God's own possession." Those are secure who bear the impress of the Spirit
of God, who are being transformed into the likeness of his
Son.

The intimation that it is only the true people of God
who are thus sealed is given by the statement that there
are twelve thousand "out of every tribe of the children of
Israel." The whole picture is symbolical. Twelve times
twelve, multiplied by one thousand, or "a hundred and
forty and four thousand" is an ideal number denoting that
the body is complete yet unlimited. As the priestly tribe
of Levi is included in the list, one tribe must be omitted
so as not to mar the symmetry of the symbolism and the
significance of the number "twelve." Just why the tribe
of Dan is the one to be left out is a mere matter of conjecture. It is quite probable that Judah is mentioned first
because it is the tribe from which came our Lord Jesus
Christ, the Head of the church. Evidently the intention of
the whole vision is to indicate the fact that "the servants
of our God," the members of the ideal church, symbolized
by the twelve tribes of Israel, form an unlimited number,
yet this number is complete in the divine register, and deliverance is assured for each and every one. Just how the
deliverance is to be wrought the vision does not set forth.

It is enough to recall the words of our Lord when he predicted the signs of coming doom: "When these things begin to come to pass, look up, and lift up your heads; because your redemption draweth nigh."

Suddenly the scene is changed, and in the second of the
parenthetic visions (Rev. 7:9-17) the reader is again
transported from earth to the court of heaven. It is a
passage of incomparable sublimity and beauty. Through
all the ages Christians have been comforted by finding here
a priceless picture of the final state of the blessed dead.
However, it should be remembered that the first application of these glorious phrases is to the triumph and the
reward of the martyrs who "come out of the great tribulation." The prophet beholds that catastrophe as impending. To encourage the church to be steadfast even amidst
its horrors, he here describes the triumph and reward of
the faithful in terms which picture the tribulation as past
and the victory of the martyrs as already achieved.

He beheld "a great multitude, which no man could
number, out of every nation and of all tribes and peoples
and tongues, standing before the throne and before the
Lamb, arrayed in white robes, and palms in their hands;
and they cry with a great voice, saying,

"Salvation unto our God who sitteth on the throne,
and unto the Lamb."

To this song of the redeemed sounds forth the response
of the angel chorus, the praises of which were heard when
the Redeemer first received the book with the seven seals.
(Ch. 5.) "They fell before the throne on their faces, and
worshipped God, saying,

"Amen: Blessing, and glory, and wisdom, and thanksgiving, and honor, and power, and might, be unto our
God for ever and ever. Amen."

One of the four and twenty elders appears, to interpret
to John the vision. He asks the question which John was
eager to voice: "These that are arrayed in the white robes,

who are they, and whence came they?" With great courtesy John admits his ignorance and asks for the interpretation of the vision.

The memorable reply is given in words familiar and precious to every Christian heart: "These are they that come out of the great tribulation, and they washed their robes, and made them white in the blood of the Lamb. Therefore [because of their triumphant faith, their divine cleansing, and the purity of their lives] are they before the throne of God; and they serve him day and night in his temple [in ceaseless worship which nightfall does not interrupt]: and he that sitteth on the throne shall spread his tabernacle over them [so that ceaseless praise is rewarded by an unbroken vision of the divine Glory]. They shall hunger no more, neither thirst any more; neither shall the sun strike upon them, nor any heat: for the Lamb that is in the midst of the throne shall be their shepherd, and shall guide them unto fountains of waters of life: and God shall wipe away every tear from their eyes."

4. THE SEVENTH SEAL Ch. 8:1

1 And when he opened the seventh seal, there followed a silence in heaven about the space of half an hour.

The "silence in heaven" which follows the opening of the seventh seal comes as a sudden surprise. The sixth seal brought us to the very end of the age, and we were expecting to see "the Son of man coming on the clouds of heaven"; but the dramatic movement was then interrupted. An episode was introduced which showed the safety and the glory of the "servants of our God." Now the dramatic action is resumed. The seventh seal is opened. Surely a voice will be heard in heaven announcing the coming and Kingdom of Christ; but instead "when he opened the seventh seal, there followed a silence in heaven."

If this "silence in heaven" had been intended as a mere

dramatic pause, even as such it would have heightened the effect and increased the eager curiosity as to what would follow. The pause is startling. Voices have been heard in heaven, the songs of seraphs, the music of harps, choirs of angels, and thunders proceeding from the throne; seven trumpets are to sound and their echoes will shake the earth; but "when he opened the seventh seal, there followed a silence in heaven." The impression of this surprise is tremendous.

However, this "silence in heaven" is far more than a literary device. It is intended to show the structure of the book. The opening of the seventh seal is followed by silence because the contents of the seventh seal are not to be revealed—not at once. "There followed a silence in heaven about the space of half an hour." This half hour denotes a brief period, and a broken period. There is an interruption; it is for a short time. "Seven trumpets" must first sound. "Seven bowls" are to be outpoured. The seven trumpets and the seven bowls are the contents of the seventh seal. Nothing could be more artistic. The prophecy moves to a great climax. Before revealing the events which the seventh seal will disclose, there is a pause and a partial review, in order that the final judgment upon that earth may be painted in more lurid colors, and the scene fully prepared for the glorious appearing of Christ. The heavens often seem silent and there is often apparent delay when God is preparing some greater deliverance, some triumph more complete.

C. THE SEVEN TRUMPETS   Chs. 8:2 to 11:19

1. INTRODUCTORY VISION: THE ANGEL AND THE INCENSE   Ch. 8:2-5

2 And I saw the seven angels that stand before God; and there were given unto them seven trumpets.

3 And another angel came and stood over the altar, having a golden censer; and there was given unto him much

incense, that he should add it unto the prayers of all the
saints upon the golden altar which was before the throne.
4 And the smoke of the incense, with the prayers of the
saints, went up before God out of the angel's hand. 5 And
the angel taketh the censer; and he filled it with the fire of
the altar, and cast it upon the earth: and there followed
thunders, and voices, and lightnings, and an earthquake.

The letters to the seven churches were preceded by the vision of Christ among the golden candlesticks. (Ch. 1.) The opening of the seven seals was introduced by the vision of Christ in the place of power. (Chs. 4; 5.) So the third great division of the book, the sounding of the seven trumpets, is opened by a prelude which portrays "the prayers of the saints." (Ch. 8:2-5.) In answer to these prayers, the trumpets are to sound. The scene is like that of the fifth seal, where the martyrs are crying out for vengeance. (Ch. 6:10.) So in this vision the prayers are a request that the judgments of God may be poured out upon his foes. Incense is, in the Bible, a familiar symbol of prayer. Here, however, another feature is included. The incense of human prayers is acceptable only when to it is added the incense of heaven, by which may be meant the intercession of Christ and the effects of his atoning work.

The scene is borrowed from the service of the Jewish tabernacle. In the Holy Place, before the veil, stood the golden altar. Daily fire was placed upon it from the altar of sacrifice, and upon the fire was poured the sacred incense. The cloud of perfume which rose and filled the room and floated beyond the veil into the holy presence chamber of God was a symbol of worship, of praise, and of prayer.

So in this vision, when the seven angels appear to whom were given the seven trumpets that were to be sounded, "another angel came and stood over the altar, having a golden censer; and there was given unto him much incense, that he should add it unto the prayers of all the saints upon the golden altar which was before the throne. And the smoke of the incense, with the prayers of the saints, went up before God out of the angel's hand."

Such a picture is an inspiration at all times, to all the followers of Christ. They always can draw near to the golden altar, and can be sure that their prayers and their praises are acceptable, because of the added incense of heaven, because of the mediation of their divine Savior and Lord. However, the prayers in this vision are of a very unusual character. They are for the vindication of the justice of God. They are for the punishment of those who have persecuted his church. Therefore, the symbol is suddenly changed. The prayers are to be answered as the seven trumpets sound. "And the angel taketh the censer; and he filled it with the fire of the altar, and cast it upon the earth." As in Ezek. 10:2, the fire of God, like coals from the altar, is cast upon the earth. Divine judgments are poured forth in response to the cry of his suffering church. "There followed thunders, and voices, and lightnings, and an earthquake." Everything is now ready for the trumpets to sound.

2. THE FIRST SIX TRUMPETS   Chs. 8:6 to 9:21

6 And the seven angels that had the seven trumpets prepared themselves to sound.

7 And the first sounded, and there followed hail and fire, mingled with blood, and they were cast upon the earth: and the third part of the earth was burnt up, and the third part of the trees was burnt up, and all green grass was burnt up.

8 And the second angel sounded, and as it were a great mountain burning with fire was cast into the sea: and the third part of the sea became blood; 9 and there died the third part of the creatures which were in the sea, even they that had life; and the third part of the ships was destroyed.

10 And the third angel sounded, and there fell from heaven a great star, burning as a torch, and it fell upon the third part of the rivers, and upon the fountains of the wa-

ters; *11 and the name of the star is called Wormwood:
and the third part of the waters became wormwood; and
many men died of the waters, because they were made
bitter.*

*12 And the fourth angel sounded, and the third part of
the sun was smitten, and the third part of the moon, and
the third part of the stars; that the third part of them should
be darkened, and the day should not shine for the third
part of it, and the night in like manner.*

*13 And I saw, and I heard an eagle, flying in mid heaven,
saying with a great voice, Woe, woe, woe, for them that
dwell on the earth, by reason of the other voices of the
trumpet of the three angels, who are yet to sound.*

*9:1 And the fifth angel sounded, and I saw a star from
heaven fallen unto the earth: and there was given to him
the key of the pit of the abyss. 2 And he opened the pit
of the abyss; and there went up a smoke out of the pit, as
the smoke of a great furnace; and the sun and the air were
darkened by reason of the smoke of the pit. 3 And out of
the smoke came forth locusts upon the earth; and power
was given them, as the scorpions of the earth have power.
4 And it was said unto them that they should not hurt the
grass of the earth, neither any green thing, neither any tree,
but only such men as have not the seal of God on their
foreheads. 5 And it was given them that they should not
kill them, but that they should be tormented five months:
and their torment was as the torment of a scorpion, when
it striketh a man. 6 And in those days men shall seek death,
and shall in no wise find it; and they shall desire to die, and
death fleeth from them. 7 And the shapes of the locusts
were like unto horses, prepared for war; and upon their
heads as it were crowns like unto gold, and their faces were
as men's faces. 8 And they had hair as the hair of women,
and their teeth were as the teeth of lions. 9 And they had
breastplates, as it were breastplates of iron; and the sound
of their wings was as the sound of chariots, of many horses
rushing to war. 10 And they have tails like unto scorpions, and stings; and in their tails is their power to hurt
men five months. 11 They have over them as king the
angel of the abyss: his name in Hebrew is Abaddon, and
in the Greek tongue he hath the name Apollyon.*

12 The first Woe is past: behold, there come yet two Woes hereafter.

13 And the sixth angel sounded, and I heard a voice from the horns of the golden altar which is before God, 14 one saying to the sixth angel that had the trumpet, Loose the four angels that are bound at the great river Euphrates. 15 And the four angels were loosed, that had been prepared for the hour and day and month and year, that they should kill the third part of men.   16 And the number of the armies of the horsemen was twice ten thousand times ten thousand: I heard the number of them.   17 And thus I saw the horses in the vision, and them that sat on them, having breastplates as of fire and of hyacinth and of brimstone: and the heads of the horses are as the heads of lions; and out of their mouths proceedeth fire and smoke and brimstone.   18 By these three plagues was the third part of men killed, by the fire and the smoke and the brimstone, which proceeded out of their mouths.   19 For the power of the horses is in their mouth, and in their tails: for their tails are like unto serpents, and have heads; and with them they hurt.   20 And the rest of mankind, who were not killed with these plagues, repented not of the works of their hands, that they should not worship demons, and the idols of gold, and of silver, and of brass, and of stone, and of wood; which can neither see, nor hear, nor walk: 21 and they repented not of their murders, nor of their sorceries, nor of their fornication, nor of their thefts.

As to the meaning of the visions which follow the sounding of the seven trumpets, there can be little doubt. The prophet is here describing the divine judgments which precede the return of Christ.   To regard the descriptions as literal predictions of actual catastrophes or to attempt to interpret the symbols in terms of specific historic or prophetic events would lead one into the sphere of the fanciful or the grotesque.   It is impossible to discover what circumstances or facts furnished to the prophet his figures of speech or the colors with which he paints his pictures of divine retribution upon an impenitent world.   However, it is evident that the punishment is not yet described as universal. Only one third of the earth or its inhabitants is affected. Then again, the purpose of the judgments is to lead men to repent. The doom here pictured is not final.

As in the case of the seven seals, so the seven trumpets are divided into two distinct groups, of four and three; and again there is a parenthetic episode between the sixth and seventh number of the series. The first four trumpets introduce judgments which, in particular, affect nature in four of its realms: the earth, the sea, the rivers, the heavenly bodies. The later trumpets concern more especially the inhabitants of the earth. Or, since nature and the well-being of men are closely related, it may be more exact to note that the last three trumpets announce judgments which are more severe, and are specified by the prophet as constituting three "Woes."

The description of these judgments corresponds in large measure to that of the plagues of Egypt. Thus when the first angel sounds there follows "hail and fire." To the Egyptian plague, however, a feature is added: the hail and fire are "mingled with blood." As a result, one third of all grass and trees is destroyed.

As the second angel sounds, a burning mountain is cast into the sea and a third part of the sea is turned into blood, thus recalling the first plague of Egypt, when the Nile became blood. As a result, a third part of the creatures in the sea and a third part of the ships are destroyed.

The bitter waters of Marah (Ex. 15:23) are recalled by the effect of the third trumpet; only the miracle is reversed. Bitter waters are not made sweet, but sweet waters are made bitter. "There fell from heaven a great star, burning as a torch, and it fell upon the third part of the rivers, and upon the fountains of the waters; and the name of the star is called Wormwood: and the third part of the waters became wormwood." Here, unlike the sounding of the first and second trumpets, a more serious result follows, namely, the loss of human life: "Many men died of the waters."

As under the ninth plague Egypt was plunged into darkness, so when the fourth angel sounds, the sun and moon and stars are smitten, so that "the day should not shine for the third part of it." This is with a view to the effect on mankind. The judgment is partial. It is designed to warn and not to destroy.

The fifth and sixth trumpets bring disaster and still more dread. They constitute two of the last three woes that are to be visited upon the earth, and they are announced as such by an eagle, "flying in mid heaven." However, the plagues of Egypt are still in view. When the fifth trumpet is sounded swarms of locusts appear. This disaster is far more terrible, however, than that which visited the land of Egypt. These locusts issue from "the pit of the abyss." They are loosed by one who has fallen from heaven, who has been given "the key of the pit," who seems to be none other than Satan. These locusts are demonic creatures. They have the power to sting like scorpions. Instead of consuming vegetation, which the hail and fire have in part destroyed, they attack men. As the Israelites were exempt from the plagues of Egypt, so those men escape who have "the seal of God on their foreheads." All others are tormented by the locusts, whose sting is like "the torment of a scorpion." Their pain is worse than the anguish of death. Indeed, "in those days men shall seek death, and shall in no wise find it."

The vision is closed with a further description of these hellish tormentors. They are shaped like horses, they have crowns of gold, their faces are like men's, they have "hair as the hair of women," they have teeth like lions'. They appear with the armor of warriors. Their most terrible feature, however, is their tails, with stings like those of scorpions. Their king is "the angel of the abyss" named "Apollyon," that is, the "Destroyer."

As the sixth angel sounds, a single voice is heard "from

the horns of the golden altar." This voice is interpreting the desire and expressing the prayer of the church. It is addressed to the angel that has the sixth trumpet: "Loose the four angels that are bound at the great river Euphrates." These four angels are the agents of divine justice, the ministers of the divine judgments. The fifth trumpet has summoned a cloud of locusts from "the pit of the abyss." The sixth trumpet summons a vast host of horsemen from the valley of the Euphrates. This great river was the eastern limit of the Land of Promise. Beyond it lay the dreaded enemies of Israel, the heathen nations of Babylon and Assyria. Isaiah (ch. 8:7) pictures an invasion of these foes as an overflow of the Euphrates. So John here describes the four angels of judgment as "bound at the great river Euphrates." When they are loosed, the flood breaks from its barrier and destruction follows.

As the Euphrates was likewise the eastern boundary of the Roman domain, many readers suppose that John here borrows his figures from a dreaded invasion by the Parthians, whose empire stretched as far to the west as the "great river."

Whatever may have suggested the imagery to the inspired writer, he pictures the work of the avenging angels as wrought by the ravages of invading armies. The judgment falls at a divinely appointed time. It "had been prepared for the hour and day and month and year." Its purpose is not only to inflict a penalty but to convey a warning to an impenitent world. Destruction is not to be complete. Power is given that they shall "kill the third part of men."

"The number of the armies of the horsemen" is astounding. It is "twice ten thousand times ten thousand," or two hundred million. The appearance of the riders is terrifying. They have breastplates whose colors are like fire and smoke and brimstone. The attention centers, however, not so much on the riders as on the horses. To the Jewish mind horses were usually objects of terror. Yet these horses, like the "locusts" summoned by the fifth trumpet, have features of preternatural horror. "The heads of the horses are as the heads of lions; and out of their mouths proceedeth fire and smoke and brimstone. . . . Their tails are like unto serpents, and have heads; and with them they hurt."

It has been supposed that John is here picturing the Parthian cavalry. What exact event of the past or future is here set forth it is impossible to conjecture. The message is absolutely clear. Punishments no matter how severe, warnings no matter how terrifying, may not avail to turn men from their worship of false gods or their practice of impurity and crime. Thus the scene of terror closes with this severe indictment: "And the rest of mankind, who were not killed with these plagues, repented not of the works of their hands, that they should not worship demons, and the idols of gold, and of silver, and of brass, and of stone, and of wood; which can neither see, nor hear, nor walk: and they repented not of their murders, nor of their sorceries, nor of their fornication, nor of their thefts."

3. EPISODE: THE LITTLE BOOK AND THE TWO WITNESSES Chs. 10:1 to 11:14

1 And I saw another strong angel coming down out of heaven, arrayed with a cloud; and the rainbow was upon his head, and his face was as the sun, and his feet as pillars of fire; 2 and he had in his hand a little book open: and he set his right foot upon the sea, and his left upon the earth; 3 and he cried with a great voice, as a lion roareth: and when he cried, the seven thunders uttered their voices. 4 And when the seven thunders uttered their voices, I was about to write: and I heard a voice from heaven saying, Seal up the things which the seven thunders uttered, and write them not. 5 And the angel that I saw standing upon the sea and upon the earth lifted up his right hand to heaven, 6 and sware by him that liveth for ever and ever, who created the heaven and the things that are therein, and the earth and the things that are therein, and the sea and the things that are therein, that there shall be delay no longer: 7 but in the days of the voice of the seventh angel, when he is about to sound, then is finished the mystery of God, according to the good tidings which he declared to his servants the prophets. 8 And the voice which I heard from heaven, I heard it again speaking with me, and saying, Go, take the book which is open in the hand of the angel that standeth upon the sea and upon the earth. 9 And I went unto the angel, saying unto him that he should give me the little book. And he saith unto me, Take it, and eat it up; and it shall make thy belly bitter, but in thy mouth it shall be sweet as honey. 10 And I took the little book out of the angel's hand, and ate it up; and it was in my mouth sweet as honey: and when I had eaten it, my belly was made bitter. 11 And they say unto me, Thou must prophesy again over many peoples and nations and tongues and kings.

11:1 And there was given me a reed like unto a rod: and one said, Rise, and measure the temple of God, and the altar, and them that worship therein. 2 And the court which is without the temple leave without, and measure it not; for it hath been given unto the nations: and the holy city shall they tread under foot forty and two months. 3 And I will give unto my two witnesses, and they shall prophesy a thousand two hundred and threescore days, clothed in sackcloth. 4 These are the two olive trees and the two candlesticks, standing before the Lord of the earth. 5 And if any man desireth to hurt them, fire proceedeth out of their mouth and devoureth their enemies; and if any man shall desire to hurt them, in this manner must he be killed. 6 These have the power to shut the heaven, that it rain not during the days of their prophecy: and they have power over the waters to turn them into blood, and to smite the earth with every plague, as often as they shall desire. 7 And when they shall have finished their testimony, the beast that cometh up out of the abyss shall make war with them, and overcome them, and kill them. 8 And their dead bodies lie in the street of the great city, which spiritually is called Sodom and Egypt, where also their Lord was crucified. 9 And from among the peoples and tribes and tongues and nations do men look upon their dead bodies three days and a half, and suffer not their dead bodies *to be laid in a tomb. 10 And they that dwell on the earth rejoice over them, and make merry; and they shall send gifts one to another; because these two prophets tormented them that dwell on the earth. 11 And after the three days and a half the breath of life from God entered into them, and they stood upon their feet; and great fear fell upon them that beheld them. 12 And they heard a great voice from heaven saying unto them, Come up hither. And they went up into heaven in the cloud; and their enemies beheld them. 13 And in that hour there was a great earthquake, and the tenth part of the city fell; and there were killed in the earthquake seven thousand persons: and the rest were affrighted, and gave glory to the God of heaven.*

14 The second Woe is past: behold, the third Woe cometh quickly.

The dramatic movement is interrupted again. As an episode was introduced between the opening of the sixth and seventh seals, so a similar interlude is introduced between the sounding of the sixth and the seventh trumpet. Both these episodes are designed to comfort the people of God. When the sixth trumpet sounded, the vast hosts of demonic horsemen seemed to threaten universal destruction. It was the second picture of woe. Following this scene, and before the seventh trumpet sounds and the third woe is announced, this parenthetic vision of the angel with the little book is given, and the testimony of the two witnesses. This vision, however, differs from the message of consolation introduced between the opening of the sixth and seventh seals. That emphasized the safety and the glory of the persecuted people of God. (Ch. 7.) This message describes a mingling of the sweet and the bitter. It speaks of persecution and tribulation, of unfaithfulness and punishment, but also of loyalty and deliverance.

The prophet sees in his inspired vision "another strong angel," not one of the seven or of the four. Nor is this a vision of Christ, as some suppose. The angel appears "coming down out of heaven," enveloped in a cloud, the

vehicle in which heavenly messengers are pictured. A
"rainbow" is "upon his head"—not the emerald circle
which John saw about the throne (ch. 4:3) but a prism of
colors appearing in the cloud and caused by the glory of
the angel's face which shone "as the sun." "His feet" are
"as pillars of fire," the symbol of strength. He sets "his
right foot upon the sea, and his left upon the earth," as
though dominating the whole world.

He has in his hand "a little book open." This is the essential feature of the vision. The "little book" is not the
sealed scroll given to the Redeemer. (Ch. 5.) It is very
small by contrast, and it is "open." In it is contained a
mere fragment of the counsels of God which are to be revealed by the prophet. Yet its contents are of deep significance. They are in substance the episode of the two witnesses which follows.

First, however, when the angel "cried with a great voice
. . . seven thunders uttered their voices." The prophet
seems to understand the meaning of these thunders and is
"about to write," when he hears "a voice from heaven
saying, Seal up the things which the seven thunders uttered, and write them not." What those utterances were
it is idle to conjecture. Evidently the prophet indicates
that he has received in his vision more than he is permitted
to reveal, or that it is now too late to record the possible
warnings of coming judgment which the "thunders" ex-
pressed. For now the angel that he saw "standing upon
the sea and upon the earth lifted up his right hand to
heaven, and sware by him that liveth for ever and ever
. . . that there shall be delay no longer." Instead of further delay, "in the days of the voice of the seventh angel,
when he is about to sound, then is finished the mystery of
God." By a "mystery" is meant something formerly concealed but now revealed. It seems here to denote "the
whole purpose of God," the joyous solution of all the
problems of history, the consummation of the divine promise of ultimate blessing for the world, which formed the

gospel—the glad tidings that God had "declared to his servants the prophets."

However, before this blessed consummation, there are to be times of great suffering for the church, and then a final deliverance. These are recorded in the little book, which the prophet is now told to take out of the hand of the angel, and not only to "take it" but to "eat it up." That is, he is to make this new revelation his own: he is to assimilate it, to identify himself with it, and to proclaim it. He is told, however, that while it will be "sweet" to his taste, yet in reality its contents will prove "bitter." It will be a joy to receive the revelation of divine purposes and to anticipate the blessings in store for the people of God, but it will be bitter to receive the predictions of the persecution and distress which the church is to endure. The picture is borrowed evidently from the experience of the prophet Ezekiel (Ezek. 3:1, 3, 14). To him the word of God was sweet, but he found much of bitterness in proclaiming the message to his people.

However, John is told that this little book does not contain the whole of his prophecy. There will be much more to disclose which will not concern his people alone but in which their fate will be involved: "And they say unto me, Thou must prophesy again over many peoples and nations and tongues and kings."

The vision (Rev. 11:1-14) which concludes the comforting episode (chs. 10:1 to 11:14) is indeed both "sweet" and "bitter." It views the people of God as bearing their faithful testimony and divinely empowered for their witness, but also suffering pain and persecution and indignity. They are delivered not *from* martyrdom and death, but *through* martyrdom and death to a glorious resurrection. The picture is presented by an almost bewildering interweaving of symbols suggested by Old Testament history and prophecy. There is reference to the Temple and altar, to Moses and Elijah, to the olive trees and the lamp stand seen by Zechariah, to the plagues upon

Pharaoh, to the tyrant predicted by Daniel, and to Sodom and Egypt and Jerusalem.

The preservation of the witnessing church is represented by the command to "measure the temple of God, and the altar, and them that worship therein." That this is a symbol of preservation and not of destruction is manifest by referring to the prophecy of Zechariah (ch. 2:1-5) from which the symbol is borrowed. The command to "rise, and measure" is addressed to John, the writer of The Revelation. He is for the time not only a spectator but an actor. This representation gives an added touch of vividness to the vision which he proceeds to relate. "The sanctuary" and "the altar" and the worshipers, the true Israel—these are to be preserved; but the unfaithful and apostate are to be "given unto the nations: and the holy city"—that is, the false as distinguished from the faithful people of God—"shall they tread under foot forty and two months." This period of time, in measurement of which a month is estimated as thirty days, is the equivalent of three years and a half, or twelve hundred and sixty days. It denotes a broken, disturbed, troubled period. It measures the tribulation caused by "the beast," who is first mentioned here (Rev. 11:7), and is the central figure in the visions which immediately follow.

At this time of distress and danger the true church will bear its faithful testimony. It is now pictured under the symbol of "two witnesses" who "shall prophesy a thousand two hundred and threescore days, clothed in sackcloth." Evidently the reference, here as in v. 6, is to Elijah and Moses. Yet this reference does not explain the full meaning of the "two witnesses" who represent the church in its divine task of testifying for Christ.

They also are called "the two olive trees and the two candlesticks, standing before the Lord of the earth"; and the reader at once goes back in memory to the vision of Zechariah (ch. 4) and is reminded of the truth that through the faithful servants of God there flows the oil of the Spirit, by whose strength they are sustained in their work and witness; as Zechariah declares, "Not by might, nor by power, but by my Spirit, saith Jehovah."

As Elijah called down fire from heaven which consumed the messengers of the king, so, somewhat changing the reference, it is said of these "two witnesses" that "if any man desireth to hurt them, fire proceedeth out of their mouth and devoureth their enemies."

As Elijah proclaimed the drought which lasted for "three years and six months" and no rain came but in answer to his prayer, so "these have the power to shut the heaven, that it rain not during the days of their prophecy." As Moses brought punishments upon the people of Egypt, so "they have power over the waters to turn them into blood, and to smite the earth with every plague, as often as they shall desire."

Thus these two witnesses were absolutely secure and irresistible until their work was done. "And when they shall have finished their testimony, the beast that cometh up out of the abyss shall make war with them, and overcome them, and kill them."

As a further indignity "their dead bodies [literally, "their dead body," picturing the whole company of the faithful] lie in the street of the great city." Thus Jerusalem, under the control of the "nations" and dominated by the "beast," has become, to the mind of the prophet, the very symbol of the godless world. It is described "spiritually," that is, "figuratively," as "Sodom," because of its moral degradation; as "Egypt," because of its cruelty and oppression; as the city "where also their Lord was crucified," because the rejection of Christ and the persecution of his people is the world's supreme offense.

The vision pictures the satanic, if childish, glee of the enemies who rejoice in the death of these two prophets. They "make merry" and "send gifts one to another." However, the defeat and the overthrow of the two witnesses is but for a brief period of time. "After the three days and a half the breath of life from God entered into them, and they stood upon their feet; and great fear fell upon them that beheld them. And they heard a great voice from heaven saying unto them, Come up hither. And they went up into heaven in the cloud; and their enemies beheld them."

By such visions the faithful witnesses for Christ have ever been sustained. All the saints and martyrs have been encouraged by the assurance of resurrection and rapture and heavenly glory. Such is still the blessed hope of the church. Such is the cheering message of the apostle Paul: "The Lord himself shall descend from heaven, with a shout, with the voice of the archangel, and with the trump of God: and the dead in Christ shall rise first; then we that are alive, that are left, shall together with them be caught up in the clouds, to meet the Lord in the air: and so shall we ever be with the Lord. Wherefore comfort one another with these words." (I Thess. 4:16-18.)

This vision of John closes with a statement of the sequel to the testimony and the ascension of the two witnesses: "In that hour there was a great earthquake, and the tenth part of the city fell; and there were killed in the earthquake seven thousand persons: and the rest were affrighted, and gave glory to the God of heaven." Such portents, such a deliverance, are not without effect. Those who have escaped are filled with terror. Many turn to God in repentance. However, there are other judgments to fall. "The second Woe is past"; this "Woe" corresponds to the sixth trumpet. "The third Woe cometh quickly"; it will follow the sounding of the seventh trumpet. Then will come the final triumph. Then the perfected reign· of Christ will begin.

4. THE SEVENTH TRUMPET   Ch. 11:15-19

15 And the seventh angel sounded; and there followed great voices in heaven, and they said,
The kingdom of the world is become the kingdom

of our Lord, and of his Christ: and he shall reign
for ever and ever.
16 And the four and twenty elders, who sit before God on
their thrones, fell upon their faces and worshipped God,
17 saying,
We give thee thanks, O Lord God, the Almighty,
who art and who wast; because thou hast taken thy
great power, and didst reign. 18 And the nations
were wroth, and thy wrath came, and the time of the
dead to be judged, and the time to give their reward
to thy servants the prophets, and to the saints, and
to them that fear thy name, the small and the great;
and to destroy them that destroy the earth.
19 And there was opened the temple of God that is in
heaven; and there was seen in his temple the ark of his
covenant; and there followed lightnings, and voices, and
thunders, and an earthquake, and great hail.

The sounding of the seventh trumpet brings to its climax the dramatic action of the book. The purposes of
God have reached their goal. His Kingdom has come "on
earth, as it is in heaven." However, speaking more exactly, this consummation has not been achieved. It is
announced. Christ has not yet appeared. Everything is
now ready for this appearing and its attendant events.
First, however, the prophet pauses. He goes back to review the origin of the church and to picture its great enemy
and the suffering it is to endure under the beast, before
Christ returns and the final triumph is complete. These
latter events will be described in the remaining portion
of The Revelation. Thus the seventh trumpet marks the
end of what is regarded rightly as the first half of the
Apocalypse (chs. 1 to 11), and it introduces the second
half of the prophecy (chs. 12 to 22).

When the seventh seal was opened, "there followed a
silence in heaven." When the seventh trumpet was
sounded, "there followed great voices in heaven, and they
said,

"The kingdom of the world is become the kingdom of our Lord, and of his Christ: and he shall reign for ever and ever."

These voices, which announce the climax of the dramatic movement, may be those of the "four living creatures" by whose praises the dramatic movement was introduced (chs. 4; 5). Their song of triumph indicates that a province, long in revolt, has been brought back beneath the sway of its rightful Sovereign and King. The rule of the Creator and of "his Christ," his Anointed, are one. Of this reign there is to be no end. When the triumphant Redeemer, having put down all enemies, delivers his perfected Kingdom to the Father (I Cor. 15:24-28), this does not exclude him from sharing his Father's throne. "Our Lord" (God) is to "reign for ever and ever," but this also is to be the reign of "his Christ."

To this outburst of praise there comes a response from the "four and twenty elders." As the "living creatures" may be symbolic of the worshiping creation, so the elders may be the ideal representatives of the redeemed. Usually they sit upon thrones even in the presence chamber of the King, but in worship they fall prostrate before him.

As they begin their anthem of adoration, one note is missing: "We give thee thanks, O Lord God, the Almighty, who art and who wast," they sing, but not, "Who art to come," for he has come. The praise is prophetic; it anticipates, it gathers into a great summary, as already accomplished, all the signal events which the future has in store: "Thou hast taken thy great power," in its final display, which centers in the return of Christ, "and didst reign." The redeemed worshipers regard that universal reign as already begun.

They view, as already past, the last great assault by a rebellious world upon the suffering church: "And the nations were wroth." But their futile hostility is met by the overwhelming judgments of God: "And thy wrath came." That "day of wrath" seems already to have come,

and with it resurrection and judgment. It is to be a day
when the Lord will reward and recompense his "prophets"
and "saints" and servants, from every rank and sphere of
life; and he will "destroy them" that now "destroy the
earth."

Suddenly the song sinks into silence and there bursts
upon the sight of the prophet a new vision of divine glory:
"There was opened the temple of God that is in heaven;
and there was seen in his temple the ark of his covenant."
The issue of all the judgments, the essence of all the rewards, is to be a more perfect access to God, a clearer
vision of his glory, a fuller understanding of his grace. All
the blessedness that the Holy Place prefigured, all the
mercy that the blood-sprinkled Ark foretold—all this was
awaiting the redeemed; all would be theirs at the coming
of the King.

"And there followed lightnings, and voices, and thunders, and an earthquake, and great hail"; for there are
divine judgments yet to fall before the Age of Gold and
the "new earth" appears.

D. THE POWERS OF EVIL   Chs. 12 to 14

1. INTRODUCTORY VISION: THE DRAGON AND
THE WOMAN   Chs. 12:1 to 13:1a

*1 And a great sign was seen in heaven: a woman arrayed
with the sun, and the moon under her feet, and upon her
head a crown of twelve stars; 2 and she was with child;
and she crieth out, travailing in birth, and in pain to be delivered. 3 And there was seen another sign in heaven: and
behold, a great red dragon, having seven heads and ten
horns, and upon his heads seven diadems. 4 And his tail
draweth the third part of the stars of heaven, and did cast
them to the earth: and the dragon standeth before the
woman that is about to be delivered, that when she is delivered he may devour her child. 5 And she was delivered
of a son, a man child, who is to rule all the nations with a
rod of iron: and her child was caught up unto God and
unto his throne. 6 And the woman fled into the wilderness,*

where she hath a place prepared of God, that there they may nourish her a thousand two hundred and threescore days.

7 And there was war in heaven: Michael and his angels going forth to war with the dragon; and the dragon warred and his angels; 8 and they prevailed not, neither was their place found any more in heaven. 9 And the great dragon was cast down, the old serpent, he that is called the Devil and Satan, the deceiver of the whole world; he was cast down to the earth, and his angels were cast down with him. 10 And I heard a great voice in heaven saying,

> *Now is come the salvation, and the power, and the kingdom of our God, and the authority of his Christ: for the accuser of our brethren is cast down, who accuseth them before our God day and night. 11 And they overcame him because of the blood of the Lamb, and because of the word of their testimony; and they loved not their life even unto death. 12 Therefore rejoice, O heavens, and ye that dwell in them. Woe for the earth and for the sea: because the devil is gone down unto you, having great wrath, knowing that he hath but a short time.*

13 And when the dragon saw that he was cast down to the earth, he persecuted the woman that brought forth the man child. 14 And there were given to the woman the two wings of the great eagle, that she might fly into the wilderness unto her place, where she is nourished for a time, and times, and half a time, from the face of the serpent. 15 And the serpent cast out of his mouth after the woman water as a river, that he might cause her to be carried away by the stream. 16 And the earth helped the woman, and the earth opened her mouth and swallowed up the river which the dragon cast out of his mouth. 17 And the dragon waxed wroth with the woman, and went away to make war with the rest of her seed, that keep the commandments of God, and hold the testimony of Jesus: 13:1 and he stood upon the sand of the sea.

The persecution from which the church has suffered is to continue and is to deepen into a "great tribulation" as the age draws to its close. This is the main fact which lies back of the entire Apocalypse. To encourage Christians to be steadfast in suffering is the very purpose of the prophecy. The first half of the book has indicated dire judgments which are to fall upon the enemies of Christ, and the ultimate safety of his followers. In the latter half of the book, the powers of evil which oppose the church are pictured with more exactness, and the triumph of Christ and the glory of his church are painted in visions of matchless splendor.

The first half of the book was divided into three sections: "The Seven Letters to the Churches of Asia"; "The Seven Seals"; "The Seven Trumpets." The second half of the book comprises four sections. Thus its opening section is the central one of the seven which mark the structure of the Apocalypse. It sets forth vividly the chief enemies of the church, under the symbols of a red dragon and two beasts. (Chs. 12 to 14.) It is followed by the sections which describe "The Seven Bowls" (chs. 15; 16); "The Triumph of Christ" (chs. 17 to 20); and "The New Jerusalem" (chs. 21:1 to 22:5).

This central section (chs. 12 to 14) is opened with an introductory vision (chs. 12:1 to 13:1a), as is the case with all the main divisions of the book. It indicates that controlling all the enemies of the church is Satan, the enemy, and that behind all the powers of evil is the evil one. The church, the true people of God, both of the Old Testament and the New, is represented as "a woman arrayed with the sun, and the moon under her feet, and upon her head a crown of twelve stars." The imagery may possibly be taken from Joseph's dream. (Gen. 37:9.) The woman represents Israel, but the ideal Israel, represented at the time of Christ's birth by such righteous ones as Zacharias and Elisabeth, Mary and Joseph, and Anna and Simeon, and in later days by the faithful followers of Christ.

This woman is about to give birth to a child, but before

her stands "a great red dragon, . . . that when she is delivered he may devour her child." The dragon is red, the
color of blood, because of his cruel malice and deadly
hate. He is pictured as "having seven heads and ten
horns, and upon his heads seven diadems," symbols of
worldwide power and sovereignty. Possibly to indicate
his prodigious size and strength, it is added, "And his tail
draweth the third part of the stars of heaven, and did cast
them to the earth." But when the woman has given birth
to a Son, "who is to rule all the nations with a rod of iron,"
her Child is "caught up unto God and unto his throne."

The reference to the peril of our Lord at the time of his
birth is plain, as is indeed the reference to his ascension;
but the gospel story is surprisingly condensed. However,
enough is said to accomplish the purpose of the prophet.
He has shown the deadly enmity of the adversary, his defeat, and the exaltation of Christ to the place of supreme
and universal power.

The wrath of Satan is now turned toward the church,
but the woman flees "into the wilderness, where she hath
a place prepared of God, that there they may nourish her
a thousand two hundred and threescore days." The picture of divine protection may be taken from the experience
of Israel in the wilderness. The period of time, elsewhere
described as "a time, and times, and half a time," or three
and one half years, indicates any period of severe persecution, but points forward to the last "great tribulation,"
from which deliverance is given by the return of Christ.

The vision then describes more fully the defeat of Satan.
His supreme effort, directed against the Son of God, results not merely in failure but in his expulsion from
heaven. Potentially, his power is gone. "The prince of
the powers of the air" has been judged, has been destroyed.
(John 12:31; Heb. 2:14.) This dethronement of Satan
has been accomplished by the birth and ministry, the death
and resurrection and ascension, of Christ. Such is the
meaning of the "war in heaven," when "the great dragon

was cast down, the old serpent, he that is called the Devil and Satan, the deceiver of the whole world; he was cast down to the earth, and his angels were cast down with him."

This victory is celebrated by celestial music, and "a great voice in heaven," sounding not only the note of triumph but of warning as well: "Now is come the salvation, and the power, and the kingdom of our God, and the authority of his Christ: for the accuser of our brethren is cast down." This salvation and victory are ascribed to the atoning death of Christ: "They overcame him because of the blood of the Lamb." Yet the sacrifice of Christ does not avail except for such as suffer with him: "They overcame . . . because of the word of their testimony; and they loved not their life even unto death."

In view of such victory, the heavens may well be glad: "Therefore rejoice, O heavens, and ye that dwell in them"; but there is "woe for the earth and for the sea." The enemy, in principle, has been destroyed, but actually he has power on earth for a season: "The devil is gone down unto you, having great wrath, knowing that he hath but a short time."

Thus the scene is again transferred to earth. The devil recognizes that his defeat is final. He is powerless against the Son, but for a time he can persecute the woman. However, she escapes into the wilderness where she is nourished during a period of great persecution. The devil attempts to prevent her escape by casting out of his mouth a flood of water; but the earth "opened her mouth and swallowed up the river." To exactly what providential deliverance from lawless and raging enemies the incident refers, it is difficult to conjecture.

The woman, however, is preserved. The most satanic attack can never destroy the church, but individual Christians can be made the victims of Satan's hatred and spite. Thus "the dragon waxed wroth with the woman, and went away to make war with the rest of her seed, that keep the commandments of God, and hold the testimony of Jesus."

On his way to the war, the dragon is pictured as halting by the shore of the sea: "He stood upon the sand of the sea." He is to summon his dread agents, in preparation for whose appearance this introductory vision (Rev. 12:1 to 13:1a) has been given.

2. THE TWO BEASTS AND THE GREAT TRIBULATION
Ch. 13:1b-18

And I saw a beast coming up out of the sea, having ten horns and seven heads, and on his horns ten diadems, and upon his heads names of blasphemy. 2 And the beast which I saw was like unto a leopard, and his feet were as the feet of a bear, and his mouth as the mouth of a lion: and the dragon gave him his power, and his throne, and great authority. 3 And I saw one of his heads as though it had been smitten unto death; and his death-stroke was healed: and the whole earth wondered after the beast; 4 and they worshipped the dragon, because he gave his authority unto the beast; and they worshipped the beast, saying, Who is like unto the beast? and who is able to war with him? 5 and there was given to him a mouth speaking great things and blasphemies; and there was given to him authority to continue forty and two months. 6 And he opened his mouth for blasphemies against God, to blaspheme his name, and his tabernacle, even them that dwell in the heaven. 7 And it was given unto him to make war with the saints, and to overcome them: and there was given to him authority over every tribe and people and tongue and nation. 8 And all that dwell on the earth shall worship him, every one whose name hath not been written from the foundation of the world in the book of life of the Lamb that hath been slain. 9 If any man hath an ear, let him hear. 10 If any man is for captivity, into captivity he goeth: if any man shall kill with the sword, with the sword must he be killed. Here is the patience and the faith of the saints.

11 And I saw another beast coming up out of the earth; and he had two horns like unto a lamb, and he spake as a

*dragon. 12 And he exerciseth all the authority of the first
beast in his sight. And he maketh the earth and them that
dwell therein to worship the first beast, whose death-stroke
was healed. 13 And he doeth great signs, that he should
even make fire to come down out of heaven upon the earth
in the sight of men. 14 And he deceiveth them that dwell
on the earth by reason of the signs which it was given him
to do in the sight of the beast; saying to them that dwell
on the earth, that they should make an image to the beast
who hath the stroke of the sword and lived. 15 And it was
given unto him to give breath to it, even to the image of
the beast, that the image of the beast should both speak,
and cause that as many as should not worship the image
of the beast should be killed. 16 And he causeth all, the
small and the great, and the rich and the poor, and the free
and the bond, that there be given them a mark on their
right hand, or upon their forehead; 17 and that no man
should be able to buy or to sell, save he that hath the mark,
even the name of the beast or the number of his name. 18
Here is wisdom. He that hath understanding, let him count
the number of the beast; for it is the number of a man: and
his number is Six hundred and sixty and six.*

The power of evil, undoubtedly, is symbolized and embodied in Satan. Yet he must have as his agents men and
human institutions. Thus, in this central scene of the
Apocalypse, he employs two terrifying figures which are
designated as "beasts." One comes "up out of the sea";
the other, "up out of the earth."

What is meant by these "beasts"? To what do they
correspond? Probably to John they pictured the imperial
power of Rome and the cult of emperor worship, which
were united to crush the infant church. They find their
counterparts whenever a despotic civil power is combined with some form of false religion. The picture will
never be completely fulfilled until it is embodied in certain
persons or movements of the last days. These are identified with "the man of sin," and the "antichrist." Their
advent seemed near to John. Their career was to be brief,

and their destruction was to be accomplished by the returning Christ.

John borrows his figures from the visions of Daniel. (Ch. 7.) The ancient prophet depicts, under the form of four beasts, a series of world empires which have to do with the fate of his own people. John combines into one the various features of the four. The beast he describes arises "out of the sea," which latter may be a symbol of the disturbed and stormy social and political conditions out of which tyrannies commonly arise. He has "ten horns and seven heads, and on his horns ten diadems, and upon his heads names of blasphemy," which depict pagan power, worldwide and complete. The beast combines the feline cruelty and dexterity of "a leopard" with the massive strength of "a bear" and the terrifying roar of "a lion." The last may picture some sudden edict of persecution against the church. "His power, and his throne, and great authority" are given him by the dragon.

A mysterious feature is now added: "I saw one of his heads as though it had been smitten unto death; and his death-stroke was healed: and the whole earth wondered after the beast." Many suppose that the reference is to the expected return from the dead of the Roman emperor Nero. The difficulty is that such a return never took place. John would hardly assign a false report as a ground for rendering universal worship. The beast which John describes actually "had been smitten" and "his death-stroke was healed." More probable is the theory that the symbol indicates an emperor who had been a persecutor as Nero was, followed by another in whom his spirit of brutal violence was reincarnate. It may be added that this figurative resurrection is contrasted with the actual resurrection of Christ, in virtue of which he has been given universal praise and power.

Such adoration indeed is granted to the beast: "They worshipped the dragon, because he gave his authority unto the beast; and they worshipped the beast, saying, Who

is like unto the beast? and who is able to war with him?"
Furthermore, "he opened his mouth for blasphemies
against God, to blaspheme his name, and his tabernacle,
even them that dwell in the heaven."

"It was given unto him to make war with the saints,
and to overcome them: and there was given to him authority over every tribe and people and tongue and nation." However, his reign is not unlimited. It continues
"forty and two months." Then he is to be destroyed.
Meanwhile the followers of Christ are not to resist. They
are to win their true victory by steadfastness and hope,
knowing that their names have been written "in the book
of life of the Lamb that hath been slain."

To these faithful sufferers comes this difficult prediction: "If any man is for captivity, into captivity he goeth:
if any man shall kill with the sword, with the sword must
he be killed. Here is the patience and the faith of the
saints."

The second beast comes "up out of the earth." In contrast with the "sea," the "earth" may depict a settled state
of law and order, conditions under which false religions
have opportunity to rise and to flourish. Such a system
or leader seems to be represented by the second beast.
He is elsewhere called "the false prophet." He is the
servant and the executive of the first beast. He does not
have heads with imperial crowns. Unlike the first beast,
he represents, not civil, but religious power. "He had two
horns like unto a lamb"; however, "he spake as a dragon."
His words and his commands are satanic in their deception
and cruelty. He receives his "authority" from the first
beast, whom he makes "the earth and them that dwell
therein to worship." To promote this worship he per-
forms spurious miracles. He imitates the works of true
prophets like Elijah, and makes "fire to come down out
of heaven." An image of the beast is made, and by some
power of magic it is given breath so that it can speak.
This image all are compelled to worship; if any refuse

such worship, they are put to death. Moreover, no man is permitted "to buy or to sell, save he that hath the mark, even the name of the beast or the number of his name" on his right hand or on his forehead. This "mark," or "the number of his name," is declared to be "Six hundred and sixty and six."

The conjectures as to the interpretation of this number have been endless. Quite commonly it is supposed to express the numerical value of the letters which compose the Hebrew name *NRON KSR,* or "Nero Kaisar." It is quite as probable that no individual is designated, but that the figures are symbolic. The number six is one short of seven, which denotes perfection; six is therefore the symbol of imperfection and of sin. If we triple the figure six, or to the number six add six, multiplied by ten and by one hundred, there may be a "number" which represents the greatest conceivable embodiment of depravity and of evil.

Such, in any event, is the character of the beast whom the false prophet compels all the world to worship. He seems to correspond to "the man of sin" predicted by Paul. (II Thess. 2:1-10.) When civil and social order have been subverted, when lawlessness prevails, when all restraints have been removed, there arises out of this state of anarchy a tyrant of demonic character and despotic power, who does indeed establish order, but only to arrogate to himself all authority divine and human and to become the embodiment of a lawlessness worse and more fatal to the nations than that out of which he arose.

The second beast is described as differing in his character. In him the priesthood of the cult of emperor worship may be symbolized. His sphere is not political but religious. By deception and cruelty he attempts to destroy the church and to substitute for Christianity the universal worship of the beast. He appears to represent "the antichrist" predicted by John rather than "the man of sin" described by Paul. "The man of sin" and "the antichrist" have been identified so commonly that it may be futile to raise the question as to whether they may be distinct. Both are opposed to Christ and his church; both are agents of the dragon. Yet the first beast is secular and imperial; the second is a "false prophet," and also a false Christ, as well as the embodiment of enmity against Christ. An antichristian spirit always has existed. In this second beast it seems to find its supreme manifestation. As John wrote in his First Epistle, "Little children, it is the last hour: and as ye heard that antichrist cometh, even now have there arisen many antichrists. . . . Who is the liar but he that denieth that Jesus is the Christ? This is the antichrist, even he that denieth the Father and the Son." (I John 2:18, 22.)

These three, the dragon, the beast, and the false prophet, form a monstrous trinity. Under their pitiless and murderous reign, the church enters the darkest hour of its tribulation and martyrdom and distress.

3. EPISODE: THE VISION OF BLESSEDNESS AND THE MESSAGES OF CHEER   Ch. 14:1-13

1 And I saw, and behold, the Lamb standing on the mount Zion, and with him a hundred and forty and four thousand, having his name, and the name of his Father, written on their foreheads. 2 And I heard a voice from heaven, as the voice of many waters, and as the voice of a great thunder: and the voice which I heard was as the voice of harpers harping with their harps: 3 and they sing as it were a new song before the throne, and before the four living creatures and the elders: and no man could learn the song save the hundred and forty and four thousand, even they that had been purchased out of the earth. 4 These are they that were not defiled with women; for they are virgins. These are they that follow the Lamb whithersoever he goeth. These were purchased from among men, to be the first fruits unto God and unto the Lamb. 5 And in their mouth was found no lie: they are without blemish.

6 And I saw another angel flying in mid heaven, having eternal good tidings to proclaim unto them that dwell on the earth, and unto every nation and tribe and tongue and people; 7 and he saith with a great voice, Fear God, and give him glory; for the hour of his judgment is come: and worship him that made the heaven and the earth and sea and fountains of waters.

8 And another, a second angel, followed, saying, Fallen, fallen is Babylon the great, that hath made all the nations to drink of the wine of the wrath of her fornication.

9 And another angel, a third, followed them, saying with a great voice, If any man worshippeth the beast and his image, and receiveth a mark on his forehead, or upon his hand, 10 he also shall drink of the wine of the wrath of God, which is prepared unmixed in the cup of his anger; and he shall be tormented with fire and brimstone in the presence of the holy angels, and in the presence of the Lamb: 11 and the smoke of their torment goeth up for ever and ever; and they have no rest day and night, they that worship the beast and his image, and whoso receiveth the mark of his name. 12 Here is the patience of the saints, they that keep the commandments of God, and the faith of Jesus.

13 And I heard a voice from heaven saying, Write, Blessed are the dead who die in the Lord from henceforth: yea, saith the Spirit, that they may rest from their labors; for their works follow with them.

Again there is an abrupt change of scene. The vision of cruel persecution is suddenly interrupted by a message of cheer. As between the sixth and the seventh seals, and as again between the sixth and the seventh trumpets, an episode was introduced, so here, when the two beasts have been described as in full career (ch. 13) before their defeat and destruction are depicted (ch. 14:14-20), there is introduced this interlude, which is designed to encourage the followers of Christ in all times of peril and distress.

As in the case of the other interludes, this consists of two parts: first, a vision of the church in glory (vs. 1-5), and secondly, the messages of three angels and of a Voice from heaven (vs. 6-13). The first part of the vision corresponds to the episode between the sixth and seventh seals. There "a hundred and forty and four thousand" of the people of God were seen "sealed" for safety, while "a great multitude, which no man could number," were seen "standing before the throne and before the Lamb, arrayed in white robes, and palms in their hands." So here, the church, in its ideal completeness and blessedness, is represented by "a hundred and forty and four thousand," who are seen, with the Lamb, "standing on the mount Zion."

That this is a scene in heaven seems to be probable. Some readers, however, suppose John to have shown here in prophetic vision the church in its ultimate destiny, the New Jerusalem established upon earth. (Chs. 21; 22.) This company of the redeemed have "written on their foreheads" the name of the Lamb and the name of his Father. Their blessedness is chanted by celestial choirs. The music which floats down "from heaven" to the ears of the prophet is, in its majestic grandeur and its heavenly harmony, "as the voice of many waters, and as the voice of a great thunder," and also "as the voice of harpers harping with their harps." The anthem is "a new song," the song of redemption, which "no man could learn . . . save the hundred and forty and four thousand, even they that had been purchased out of the earth." Only the redeemed can understand what redemption really means.

In their ideal purity the redeemed are pictured as "virgins." They have remained true to their Lord, and have not been led away by the allurements of idolatry and the worship of the beast.

As in the first interlude of cheer it was said of the white-robed multitude that "the Lamb that is in the midst of the throne shall be their shepherd, and shall guide them unto fountains of waters of life," so here we read, "These are they that follow the Lamb whithersoever he goeth." Such is the picture of blessed and perfected fellowship with Christ.

They are martyrs, presented to God as a sacrifice and accepted as his peculiar possession, "purchased from among men, to be the first fruits unto God and unto the Lamb."

"In their mouth was found no lie," in striking contrast to the beast and the false prophet whom they had defied. "They are without blemish," like the ideal church described by Paul, "not having spot or wrinkle or any such thing."

As a further encouragement to those who are facing suffering for the sake of Christ, there come the messages of three angels and of "a voice from heaven." The first angel is seen "flying in mid heaven, having eternal good tidings to proclaim unto them that dwell on the earth." There is a question as to the content of the "good tidings." Many suppose it to be the gospel, "an eternal gospel." It rather seems to be more specifically the tidings of the changeless justice and unfailing mercy of God, the announcement that his judgment is about to fall on the guilty, and the appeal to repent before the fatal hour strikes. This is the solemn word: "Fear God, and give him glory; for the hour of his judgment is come: and worship him that made the heaven and the earth and sea and fountains of waters."

As the first angel announced impending judgment, so "a second angel" speaks as though judgment had already fallen. He anticipates the doom of Babylon, which is described at length in later visions (chs. 17; 18), and he justifies that doom: "Fallen, fallen is Babylon the great." The reason for her fall is this: she "hath made all the nations to drink of the wine of the wrath of her fornication."

"The wine" of Babylon probably means the intoxicating allurements of her luxuries and her idolatries. Yet it is also "the wine of the wrath of God," for the nations misled by the influence of Babylon are to share in her judgment and her doom.

"Babylon" is thus suddenly introduced, without any

explanation, as a symbol which John supposed all his readers would understand. This he did in the case of "the beast," in a previous parenthesis (ch. 11:7). He mentioned the symbol and then gave a full description of the beast in a subsequent vision (ch. 13).

"Babylon" probably was accepted by the early Christians as a synonym for Rome, and may be regarded in the Apocalypse as the symbol of the worldly and godless spirit which in any age makes men unfaithful to Christ and indifferent to his claims. As in the past, so in the future, any city or system or society animated by that spirit must drink inevitably of "the wine of the wrath of God."

The words of the third angel continue the predictions of doom. They are in particular a warning against the worship of "the beast and his image" and against receiving his mark on the forehead or the hand. These words paint the most dreadful picture of punishment to be found in the entire Scriptures. "The wine of the wrath of God" must be drunk when, with no ingredients of mercy, it is "prepared unmixed in the cup of his anger." The guilty "shall be tormented with fire and brimstone in the presence of the holy angels, and in the presence of the Lamb: and the smoke of their torment goeth up for ever and ever; and they have no rest day and night."

No one can read these terrible words without shuddering and questioning and dismay. It must be remembered that they are figures of speech. "The wrath of God" is his holy hatred of sin; it has nothing in common with human anger or passion. The "fire and brimstone" and "smoke of . . . torment" are taken from the story of Sodom. The suffering, "in the presence of the holy angels, and . . . of the Lamb," is in comparison with the agonies of those who endure martyrdom at the stake or in the amphitheater before multitudes of heartless spectators. These all are figures of speech, but they represent realities which are more and not less terrible than the symbols. They can hardly fail of their purpose for all who read them, and that purpose is to induce absolute loyalty to Christ and to guard against all temptations to turn aside from him, no matter what the allurements or threats of his enemies.

In view of all that the beast endeavors to inflict upon the followers of Christ, the prophet sees in these persecutions an opportunity for the church to show its steadfastness and its loyalty: "Here is the patience of the saints, they that keep the commandments of God, and the faith of Jesus."

The warning of unequaled severity which the third angel has given is followed by a promise of almost incomparable beauty which is conveyed by "a voice from heaven": "Write, Blessed are the dead who die in the Lord from henceforth: yea, saith the Spirit, that they may rest from their labors; for their works follow with them." These words are full of comfort in relation to the death of any follower of Christ in any age and place; yet it may be well to remember that their first application was to the Christian martyrs who were to suffer in "the great tribulation" under the beast. Their death "in the Lord" would be like that of their crucified Savior, as they bore witness to his name and were sustained by his grace. Their rest was not merely from the usual tasks of life, but from its hardships, its persecution, and its pain. Their reward was in "their works," in the character acquired, in the influence exerted, in the results attained, all of which would follow these martyrs into the life beyond.

4. THE HARVEST AND THE VINTAGE
Ch. 14:14-20

14 And I saw, and behold, a white cloud; and on the cloud I saw one sitting like unto a son of man, having on his head a golden crown, and in his hand a sharp sickle. 15 And another angel came out from the temple, crying with a great voice to him that sat on the cloud, Send forth thy sickle, and reap: for the hour to reap is come; for the harvest of the earth is ripe. 16 And he that sat on the cloud cast his sickle upon the earth; and the earth was reaped.

17 And another angel came out from the temple which is in heaven, he also having a sharp sickle. 18 And another angel came out from the altar, he that hath power over fire; and he called with a great voice to him that had the sharp sickle, saying, Send forth thy sharp sickle, and gather the clusters of the vine of the earth; for her grapes are fully ripe. 19 And the angel cast his sickle into the earth, and gathered the vintage of the earth, and cast it into the winepress, the great winepress, of the wrath of God. 20 And the winepress was trodden without the city, and there came out blood from the winepress, even unto the bridles of the horses, as far as a thousand and six hundred furlongs.

Here the central section of the Apocalypse (chs. 12 to 14) reaches its climax. It has pictured the powers of evil, embodied in the dragon and the two beasts, persecuting the church. Here is the description of the deliverance of the church and the destruction of her enemies. The deliverance is presented under the symbol of a "harvest"; the destruction is pictured as a "vintage" and a treading of the "winepress . . . of the wrath of God."

The harvest is gathered by the returning Christ. Again and again during the course of the prophecy he has been about to appear. From the very first his promise has been heard: "I come quickly." Now at length, when the darkest hour of need has overshadowed the church, he is seen, in prophetic vision, "like unto a son of man." He is sitting on "a white cloud." He has on his head a victor's crown of gold. He holds "in his hand a sharp sickle." A voice from the heavenly sanctuary sounds out the cry, "Send forth thy sickle, and reap: for the hour to reap is come." This hour, which has been hidden from all save the Father himself, has now arrived, the hour for which the church has been watching and praying, the hour for which the church has been made ready even by suffering; for now "the harvest of the earth is ripe." The figures of speech have been made familiar to readers of the New Testament by the parables of the sower, and of the wheat and the tares; and even more definitely by the preaching of John the Baptist, who predicted a time when One "mightier" than himself would "gather his wheat into the garner" but would "burn up" the chaff "with unquenchable fire."

The gathering of the wheat finds its counterpart in this apocalyptic vision of the harvest. For the burning of the chaff, however, another striking picture is substituted. This is the vision of the vintage. There is a delicate distinction in the figures employed. Christ himself comes to gather his loved ones to himself; but in the execution of wrath an agent is employed, an angel which comes "out from the temple which is in heaven," also "having a sharp sickle."

The command is given: "Send forth thy sharp sickle, and gather the clusters of the vine of the earth; for her grapes are fully ripe." The vine represents here a rank growth of human sin and wickedness, which must be brought under the judgment of God. The picture of judgment is painted in lurid colors of Oriental imagery. "The winepress was trodden without the city," that is, outside the true city of God. From such judgment the church is wholly exempt. The harvest already has ended. Now the winepress is trodden and the result is appalling: "There came out blood from the winepress, even unto the bridles of the horses, as far as a thousand and six hundred furlongs." The figure denotes complete and worldwide tragedy. It is the last stroke in the dramatic picture of the rise and the reign and the overthrow of the powers of evil. (Chs. 12 to 14.) These powers under the dominance of the dragon had attained universal sway; now they are overwhelmed in universal ruin. The church had been subjected to tribulation and shame; now the church shares in the glory of the triumphant Redeemer and Lord. Such pictures can never fail to give new courage and strength to the distressed followers of Christ, no matter in what age or from what source their sufferings may come. When the hour is darkest they look most confidently for the appearing of the Savior and King.

E. THE SEVEN BOWLS   Chs. 15; 16

1. INTRODUCTORY VISION: THE OVERCOMERS AND THE SEVEN ANGELS   Ch. 15

1 And I saw another sign in heaven, great and marvellous, seven angels having seven plagues, which are the last, for in them is finished the wrath of God.

2 And I saw as it were a sea of glass mingled with fire; and them that come off victorious from the beast, and from his image, and from the number of his name, standing by the sea of glass, having harps of God. 3 And they sing the song of Moses the servant of God, and the song of the Lamb, saying,

Great and marvellous are thy works, O Lord God, the Almighty; righteous and true are thy ways, thou King of the ages. 4 Who shall not fear, O Lord, and glorify thy name? for thou only art holy; for all the nations shall come and worship before thee; for thy righteous acts have been made manifest.

5 And after these things I saw, and the temple of the tabernacle of the testimony in heaven was opened: 6 and there came out from the temple the seven angels that had the seven plagues, arrayed with precious stone, pure and bright, and girt about their breasts with golden girdles. 7 And one of the four living creatures gave unto the seven angels seven golden bowls full of the wrath of God, who liveth for ever and ever. 8 And the temple was filled with smoke from the glory of God, and from his power; and none was able to enter into the temple, till the seven plagues of the seven angels should be finished.

In the preceding chapter, Christ has appeared in glory; he has gathered the wheat into his garner; judgment is

come and the wicked have been trodden in "the winepress
. . . of the wrath of God." Now we naturally expect the
picture of the new heaven and the new earth, and the
splendor of the perfected Kingdom of Christ. But again
there is a pause. There appears as a surprise a new series
of judgments. As is the plan of the prophet, he reviews,
he recapitulates, he enlarges upon the scene he already has
sketched. He shows more in detail what the seventh seal
has disclosed and what the seventh trumpet has announced.
He presents under entirely different imagery what "the
winepress . . . of the wrath of God" may denote. He
does so by the symbolism of the emptying out of "seven
golden bowls full of the wrath of God."

However, as in every one of the seven main divisions of
the prophecy, the dramatic action is preceded by an introductory vision (ch. 15). This vision is for the comfort and encouragement of the church, which is to be delivered from the wrath of God. Thus before the scenes of
judgment there is a picture of the church in glory. The
particular reference is to the blessedness of the martyrs
who have suffered under the persecution of the beast; but
in such a picture there is a place for all the true people of
God who have conquered in the struggle against evil and
have entered upon their heavenly joys.

This introductory vision opens with the appearance in
heaven of "seven angels having seven plagues, which are
the last, for in them is finished the wrath of God." However, before these angels are given power to execute judgment the attention of the prophet is turned toward a scene
in heaven.

He beholds the great company of the redeemed. They
are described as those "that come off victorious from the
beast, and from his image, and from the number of his
name." They are standing by "a sea of glass mingled with
fire." They have "harps of God. And they sing the song
of Moses the servant of God, and the song of the Lamb."
The reader is transported in memory to the scenes of the

exodus. He beholds Israel, redeemed from bondage, standing on the farther shore of the Red Sea. The surface of the waters is reddened by the light of the pillar of fire. Beneath the waves the hosts of Pharaoh lie engulfed. To the sound of the timbrel the song of deliverance is being raised: "I will sing unto Jehovah, for he hath triumphed gloriously."

Yet the song that the prophet now hears in heaven is not only the song of Moses. It is also "the song of the Lamb." It is the song of completed redemption, the song of the universal church. And as the seer listens to the song, it swells into an anthem which celebrates the final judgments, the unlimited power, and the universal sway of the King of kings:

> "Great and marvellous are thy works, O Lord God, the Almighty; righteous and true are thy ways, thou King of the ages. Who shall not fear, O Lord, and glorify thy name? for thou only art holy; for all the nations shall come and worship before thee; for thy righteous acts have been made manifest."

As the strains of praise sink into silence, the attention of the prophet is turned again to the agents of divine judgment. He sees "the temple of the tabernacle of the testimony in heaven." The reference to the tables of the law, "the testimony," intimates the holiness and justice of God, whose judgment is to be executed. The "temple" is "opened"; and out from the Holy of Holies, from the very presence chamber of God, issue "the seven angels" that have "the seven plagues."

They are pictured as "arrayed with precious stone, pure and bright, and girt about their breasts with golden girdles." The garb is royal and priestly like that in the vision of the Son of Man. (Ch. 1:13.) All the garments of the angels are studded with jewels, as though they are "arrayed with precious stone." Their ministry is priestly, although involving such severity and duties so dreadful.

Now they are given power for the execution of their task. "One of the four living creatures gave unto the seven angels seven golden bowls full of the wrath of God." The "living creatures," which appear again and again in the course of The Revelation, have been described already as the representatives of creation. The forces of nature thus are regarded as the ministers of divine judgment. The instruments of punishment are declared to be "seven golden bowls full of the wrath of God." The word for "bowls," often translated "vials," denotes vessels which are broad and shallow, rather than narrow and deep. They correspond to the basins of the Old Testament sanctuary, used for carrying incense. They were vessels so shaped that their contents could be emptied easily and completely. These bowls are filled with the wrath of God. Their burning contents are about to be poured out upon the earth.

To complete the terror and the mystery of the scene, "the temple was filled with smoke from the glory of God, and from his power; and none was able to enter into the temple, till the seven plagues of the seven angels should be finished." So it was of old. Smoke covered Mt. Sinai when the law was given there (Ex. 19:18); "the cloud filled the house" when the tabernacle was erected and when the Temple was dedicated (I Kings 8:10-11); and "the house was filled with smoke" when Isaiah was granted his vision (Isa. 6:4). This was a symbol of divine majesty. Here the smoke proceeds "from the glory of God, and from his power." It expresses his holiness and his might. Well may a wicked world stand in awe of him. Nor can anyone understand his judgments until they are fulfilled and have achieved their ultimate and glorious purpose. None could "enter into the temple, till the seven plagues . . . should be finished."

2. THE FIRST SIX BOWLS   Ch. 16:1-12

1 And I heard a great voice out of the temple, saying to the seven angels, Go ye, and pour out the seven bowls of the wrath of God into the earth.

2 And the first went, and poured out his bowl into the earth; and it became a noisome and grievous sore upon the men that had the mark of the beast, and that worshipped his image.

3 And the second poured out his bowl into the sea; and it became blood as of a dead man; and every living soul died, even the things that were in the sea.

4 And the third poured out his bowl into the rivers and the fountains of the waters; and it became blood. 5 And I heard the angel of the waters saying, Righteous art thou, who art and who wast, thou Holy One, because thou didst thus judge: 6 for they poured out the blood of saints and prophets, and blood hast thou given them to drink: they are worthy. 7 And I heard the altar saying, Yea, O Lord God, the Almighty, true and righteous are thy judgments.

8 And the fourth poured out his bowl upon the sun; and it was given unto it to scorch men with fire. 9 And men were scorched with great heat: and they blasphemed the name of God who hath the power over these plagues; and they repented not to give him glory.

10 And the fifth poured out his bowl upon the throne of the beast; and his kingdom was darkened; and they gnawed their tongues for pain, 11 and they blasphemed the God of heaven because of their pains and their sores; and they repented not of their works.

12 And the sixth poured out his bowl upon the great river, the river Euphrates; and the water thereof was dried up, that the way might be made ready for the kings that come from the sunrising.

The pouring out of the seven bowls depicts the final judgments of God upon the enemies of Christ and his church. The symbols in large part are drawn from the story of the plagues of Egypt and have a close correspondence to those which appear in this prophecy in connection with the sounding of the seven trumpets. The series of bowls and the series of trumpets, however, are not strictly parallel. There are resemblances, but the differences are even more significant. The plagues introduced by the trumpets affected only one third of the earth and sea, the streams, and the lights of heaven; the plagues which flow from the bowls are total in their effect. The first four trumpets inflicted no suffering upon mankind, but from the first the bowls bring punishment to guilty men. The trumpets constituted a call to repentance; the bowls are the outpouring of the wrath of God. During the sounding of the trumpets the church was on earth, and bearing its witness for Christ; before the bowls are outpoured, and before the world is visited with the seven last plagues, the church has been removed from the scene. The harvest has occurred before the vintage. (Ch. 14:14-20.) The redeemed are singing by the "sea of glass," before the appearance of "the seven angels," to whom were given the "seven golden bowls full of the wrath of God."

The first angel "poured out his bowl into the earth"; and the effect is like the sixth Egyptian plague: "It became a noisome and grievous sore upon the men that had the mark of the beast, and that worshipped his image."

"The second poured out his bowl into the sea; and it became blood as of a dead man; and every living soul died, even the things that were in the sea.

"And the third poured out his bowl into the rivers and the fountains of the waters; and it became blood." All this is like the first plague of Egypt, but by it only the Nile was affected. This is like the result of the second trumpet, but by it only "the third part of the sea became blood"; or like the issue of the third trumpet, but then only "the third part of the rivers" was involved and became "bitter."

Unlike the narrative of the trumpet, two voices are now heard explaining why all the waters have been turned into blood. "The angel of the waters" bears witness to the fact that this plague is a judgment of God, and that it is a just judgment: "Righteous art thou, who art and who wast, thou Holy One, because thou didst thus judge: for they poured out the blood of saints and prophets, and blood hast thou given them to drink: they are worthy"!

To the confession of those upon whom the judgment falls comes the response from those on whose account the judgment has been inflicted. These latter are the prophets and martyrs, whose prayers and praises come from "the altar": "Yea, O Lord God, the Almighty, true and righteous are thy judgments."

When the fourth trumpet sounded "the third part of the sun was . . . darkened," but now, when the fourth bowl is poured out, the heat of the sun is made more intense. It becomes a source of torment: "And men were scorched with great heat."

However, the result of the plague is not repentance. As "Pharaoh's heart was hardened," so those upon whom this judgment has fallen "blasphemed the name of God who hath the power over these plagues; and they repented not."

The fifth bowl is "poured out . . . upon the throne of the beast." Until now the plagues have overwhelmed the followers of the beast; now judgment falls upon the monster himself. The seat of the world power is assailed. "His kingdom was darkened." It must not be understood that darkness is the only punishment inflicted upon the capital of the godless empire, nor must it be supposed that the effects of the previous plagues have ceased. On the contrary, the pain of the "grievous sore" and the scorching heat of the sun continue. The darkness is the dread precursor of death.

Yet this plague produces no moral change. Men are driven into deeper sin. "They gnawed their tongues for pain, and they blasphemed the God of heaven because of their pains and their sores; and they repented not of their works."

The sixth bowl is "poured out . . . upon the great

river, the river Euphrates; and the water thereof was dried up." The purpose of this is "that the way might be made ready for the kings that come from the sunrising." The Euphrates was regarded by the Roman world as its eastern boundary and as a barrier against the incursion of hostile tribes. To dry up the water of the river was to transform it into a broad, open way for the invasion of overwhelming armies from the East.

It may be noted that at the sounding of the sixth trumpet four angels were released, who set in motion an innumerable host of destructive horsemen. Thus the pouring out of the sixth bowl results in the removal of a barrier and makes possible the onrush of "the kings of the whole world," who are gathered for the conflict with Christ and his followers.

3. EPISODE: THE GATHERING OF THE KINGS
Ch. 16:13-16

13 And I saw coming *out of the mouth of the dragon, and out of the mouth of the beast, and out of the mouth of the false prophet, three unclean spirits, as it were frogs: 14 for they are spirits of demons, working signs; which go forth unto the kings of the whole world, to gather them together unto the war of the great day of God, the Almighty. 15 (Behold, I come as a thief. Blessed is he that watcheth, and keepeth his garments, lest he walk naked, and they see his shame.) 16 And they gathered them together into the place which is called in Hebrew Har-Magedon.*

As in the case of the seven seals and of the seven trumpets, there was an interruption between the sixth and the seventh of the series, so here between the pouring out of the sixth and the seventh bowls there occurs a brief parenthetic episode.

This episode makes plain the process and the purpose and the place of the gathering of "the kings of the whole world." These kings are gathered by the influence of the three chief enemies of Christ and his church. They have appeared before in the course of this prophecy. They form the monstrous trinity of evil—the dragon, the beast, and the false prophet. The former is called "the old serpent, . . . the Devil and Satan" (ch. 12:9). To him can be traced ultimately all opposition to Christ and his cause. He has as his agents the beast and the false prophet. The former is the "beast coming up out of the sea," unto whom "it was given . . . to make war with the saints" and to hold "authority over every tribe and people and tongue and nation" (ch. 13:1, 7).

The false prophet is, beyond question, the second beast which was seen "coming up out of the earth," apparently the representative of godless religious power who compelled all men to "worship the image of the beast," the satanic political despot. These three exercise their influence by means of "three unclean spirits, as it were frogs" (ch. 16:13). From the mouth of each of these goes forth one such spirit. The mouth is the symbol of persuasive speech. To the mind of the prophet the frog represented uncleanness. Thus impure impulses, and possibly satanic malice, lust for political power, and the bitterness of religious fanaticism unite to precipitate a war involving the whole world. Thus the kings are gathered "together unto the war of the great day of God, the Almighty." So the purpose of this vast marshaling of forces is to oppose God and his omnipotent power. This is the preparation for the last great battle between good and evil, between right and wrong, between Christ and the dragon.

The mention of "the great day of God" causes the prophet to break the thread of his report and to insert a message intended to emphasize the nearness of that great day and the need of watchfulness on the part of the followers of Christ. It is as though Christ himself were speaking to the reader: "Behold, I come as a thief. Blessed is he that watcheth, and keepeth his garments, lest he walk naked, and they see his shame." To come "as a thief" means to come suddenly and unannounced. A blessing, one of "the seven beatitudes of the Apocalypse," is pronounced upon one who shows constant, wakeful vigilance, like a sentinel on duty. One who "keepeth his garments" is one who does not take them off and go to sleep. Otherwise he might "walk naked" if suddenly aroused and compelled to flee unclad. His would be the shame of having been found asleep and off his guard. This is the explanation of many a lost battle, many a moral defeat.

To the mind of Christ, his triumphant return and the final conflict with evil was ever near; and he bids his servants to watch and to be ready, as they know not at what hour their Lord may come.

The place of the final conflict is described by a symbol that is full of meaning: "They gathered them together into the place which is called in Hebrew Har-Magedon." The name denotes the hill, or the city, or the water, of Megiddo. This battlefield in the Plain of Esdraelon was a historic scene of slaughter. There Barak and Deborah overthrew the kings of Canaan, and there Josiah met his defeat and death. The mourning for Josiah in the valley of Megiddo was ever remembered as a typical instance of national grief. (Zech. 12:11.) Thus Har-Magedon properly designates a place of death and slaughter. It predicts the complete destruction of the hosts which the demonic spirits gather for that last great conflict which issues in the universal triumph of Christ.

4. THE SEVENTH BOWL   Ch. 16:17-21

17 And the seventh poured out his bowl upon the air; and there came forth a great voice out of the temple, from the throne, saying, It is done: 18 and there were lightnings, and voices, and thunders; and there was a great earthquake, such as was not since there were men upon the earth, so great an earthquake, so mighty. 19 And the great city was divided into three parts, and the cities of the nations fell:

*and Babylon the great was remembered in the sight of God,
to give unto her the cup of the wine of the fierceness of his
wrath. 20 And every island fled away, and the mountains
were not found. 21 And great hail, every stone about the
weight of a talent, cometh down out of heaven upon men:
and men blasphemed God because of the plague of the hail;
for the plague thereof is exceeding great.*

The seventh bowl is "poured out . . . upon the air,"
the atmosphere which all must breathe, the sphere of dis-
turbances by which human health and life are endangered.
This plague is of more deadly consequence than the smit-
ing of the earth or sea or rivers or even the sun. As the
bowl is emptied, there comes a voice from the heavenly
sanctuary, and from the throne of God, saying, "It is
done." The series now is complete. With the contents
of this seventh bowl the "seven plagues, which are the
last," will be ended.

The announcement is attended by "lightnings, and
voices, and thunders," the usual accompaniments of divine
judgments. Then follows "a great earthquake, such as
was not since there were men upon the earth." As a consequence, "the great city was divided into three parts, and
the cities of the nations fell." The "city," in the view of
the prophet, probably was Rome, yet Rome as the symbol of godlessness and impurity, the city identified with
"Babylon the great," which is now "remembered in the
sight of God, to give unto her the cup of the wine of the
fierceness of his wrath."

Furthermore, the islands and mountains flee away; and,
as the climax of the plague, "great hail, every stone about
the weight of a talent," a weight of more than one hundred pounds, "cometh down out of heaven upon men."
Yet as a consequence of even such terrific punishments
there is no repentance. The results are the same as under
the impact of the fourth and fifth of these plagues: "Men
blasphemed God because of the plague of the hail; for the
plague thereof is exceeding great."

It would be difficult to interpret the content of these

bowls as literal convulsions of nature, and quite as difficult to find corresponding events of history either in the future or in the past. They are symbolic pictures of final and comprehensive judgments upon the enemies of God. Yet they indicate in mere outline what is set forth in detail by the visions which now follow. The kings have been summoned for the battle of Har-Magedon, which is yet to be described. "Babylon" has come into remembrance "in the sight of God," and the destruction of this great city is to be the most impressive of all the pictures of punishment and doom which fill the following visions (chs. 17 to 20) and prepare for the closing scenes of splendor, the glories of the new heaven and the new earth (chs. 21:1 to 22:5).

F. THE TRIUMPH OF CHRIST   Chs. 17 to 20

1. INTRODUCTORY VISION: BABYLON AND THE BEAST   Ch. 17

1 And there came one of the seven angels that had the seven bowls, and spake with me, saying, Come hither, I will show thee the judgment of the great harlot that sitteth upon many waters; 2 with whom the kings of the earth committed fornication, and they that dwell in the earth were made drunken with the wine of her fornication. 3 And he carried me away in the Spirit into a wilderness: and I saw a woman sitting upon a scarlet-colored beast, full of names of blasphemy, having seven heads and ten horns. 4 And the woman was arrayed in purple and scarlet, and decked with gold and precious stone and pearls, having in her hand a golden cup full of abominations, even the unclean things of her fornication, 5 and upon her forehead a name written, MYSTERY, BABYLON THE GREAT, THE MOTHER OF THE HARLOTS AND OF THE ABOMINATIONS OF THE EARTH. 6 And I saw the woman drunken with the blood of the saints, and with the blood of the martyrs of Jesus. And when I saw her, I wondered with a great wonder. 7 And the angel said unto me, Wherefore didst thou

*wonder? I will tell thee the mystery of the woman, and
of the beast that carrieth her, which hath the seven heads
and the ten horns. 8 The beast that thou sawest was, and
is not; and is about to come up out of the abyss, and to
go into perdition. And they that dwell on the earth shall
wonder, they whose name hath not been written in the book
of life from the foundation of the world, when they behold
the beast, how that he was, and is not, and shall come. 9
Here is the mind that hath wisdom. The seven heads are
seven mountains, on which the woman sitteth: 10 and they
are seven kings; the five are fallen, the one is, the other is
not yet come; and when he cometh, he must continue a
little while. 11 And the beast that was, and is not, is himself also an eighth, and is of the seven; and he goeth into
perdition. 12 And the ten horns that thou sawest are ten
kings, who have received no kingdom as yet; but they receive authority as kings, with the beast, for one hour. 13
These have one mind, and they give their power and authority unto the beast. 14 These shall war against the
Lamb, and the Lamb shall overcome them, for he is Lord
of lords, and King of kings; and they also shall overcome
that are with him, called and chosen and faithful. 15 And
he saith unto me, The waters which thou sawest, where the
harlot sitteth, are peoples, and multitudes, and nations, and
tongues. 16 And the ten horns which thou sawest, and the
beast, these shall hate the harlot, and shall make her desolate and naked, and shall eat her flesh, and shall burn her
utterly with fire. 17 For God did put in their hearts to do
his mind, and to come to one mind, and to give their kingdom unto the beast, until the words of God should be accomplished. 18 And the woman whom thou sawest is the
great city, which reigneth over the kings of the earth.*

The Revelation is a book of cheer. It is an appeal to
faith. It is a prophecy of the final victory of Christ over
all his foes. These facts cannot be stated too frequently.
Yet it must not be forgotten that the foes of Christ are
very real. Their power and their cruel hatred are appalling. Among these enemies those most prominent in the
prophecy are the dragon, the beast, and "Babylon the

great." It is fitting, therefore, that the section in which the dramatic action reaches its climax should open with an introductory vision of Babylon and the beast (ch. 17); should paint in lurid colors the doom of Babylon (ch. 18); should depict most vividly the triumphant appearing of Christ and the overthrow of the beast (ch. 19); and should close with a vision in which the dragon, the chief of all foes, not only is "bound," but is destroyed (ch. 20).

This introductory vision of Babylon and the beast is linked to the preceding prophecy of judgments by the statement, "There came one of the seven angels that had the seven bowls, and spake with me, saying, Come hither, I will show thee the judgment of the great harlot that sitteth upon many waters." However, the actual judgment upon the "harlot," Babylon, is not seen in this preliminary vision. Here Babylon and the beast are portrayed, their relation is defined, and their destruction is predicted.

Twice before in the visions of the Apocalypse, Babylon has been mentioned. (Chs. 14:8; 16:19.) In each instance her fall has been foretold. Yet in neither place has she been described or her identity disclosed. Here she is painted in colors highly figurative and repellent. She is pictured as "a woman sitting upon a scarlet-colored beast." She is "arrayed in purple and scarlet, and decked with gold and precious stone and pearls, having in her hand a golden cup full of abominations." Upon her forehead is written her mystical name, "BABYLON THE GREAT, THE MOTHER OF THE HARLOTS AND OF THE ABOMINATIONS OF THE EARTH." She is "drunken with the blood of the saints, and with the blood of the martyrs of Jesus."

The "woman," evidently, is Rome, yet specifically neither pagan nor papal Rome but imperial Rome, as the type of every city or system which is godless, cruel, idolatrous, and opposed to Christ. The very symbol, "Babylon," is significant. That ancient city on the Euphrates was the historic and heartless enemy of Israel. It was an embodiment of luxury and license, of abominable idolatry

and unbridled impurity. No name could comprehend
more fully all the corrupting and seducing influences, all
the false religion and bloody tyranny, which John associated with the city of the Caesars.

How far such a picture of paganism and apostasy and
murderous persecution has been realized in the past, or
what exact form it may assume in the future, it would be
difficult to affirm. However, it must be noted that the
most dreadful feature of the vision is that it views the
woman as carried by the beast with "the seven heads and
the ten horns," the beast whose career was described in an
earlier chapter (ch. 13), the beast which "was, and is not;
and is about to come up out of the abyss, and to go into
perdition."

The prophet proceeds to describe further and identify
this beast. "The seven heads are seven mountains, on
which the woman sitteth: and they are seven kings; the
five are fallen, the one is, the other is not yet come." The
beast is "an eighth, and is of the seven; and he goeth into
perdition." And the "ten horns" are "ten kings," who "receive authority as kings, with the beast, for one hour."

Whence does John borrow his symbolism? What do
the symbols mean? For the source of the symbols one
needs to look quite as carefully into The Book of Daniel
as into the history of Rome. Even then it seems impossible to determine whether the "seven kings" refer to
"seven empires" or "seven emperors." The beast seems
to correspond to the "little horn" of Daniel. The statement that he "was, and is not; and is about to come up out
of the abyss" would probably indicate that he will re-
embody the cruelty and power of a previous one of "the
seven." He is in this sense one of the seven come to life
again. He is the seventh in the series, and is for a time
supported by "ten kings," who reign "with the beast, for
one hour." Yet he "is himself also an eighth," or may be
so regarded when he becomes the sole embodiment of
world power.

As seven indicates completeness, and as ten is the world number, this mysterious passage apparently means that the beast as a political or civil power is to be absolutely and universally supreme. However, as the vision opens, "Babylon" is seen sitting upon the beast. As the vision closes, we are told that "the woman," Babylon, is "the great city, which reigneth over the kings of the earth." Thus it appears that, for a time, the political world power is in league with the pagan, apostate, idolatrous city. Babylon even controls the beast.

There is, however, a sudden change of scene. Babylon is destroyed by the beast: "And the ten horns which thou sawest, and the beast, these shall hate the harlot, and shall make her desolate and naked, and shall eat her flesh, and shall burn her utterly with fire." So it appears that when the apostate, idolatrous, religious system shall have served the purpose of the beast, it will be overthrown by the beast and his confederates. Thus, if the beast is the same as the "man of sin," of whom Paul writes, it will be his final purpose to destroy all forms of religion, demanding that he himself shall be worshiped "as God" (II Thess. 2:3-4).

However, his career is brief. According to Paul, "the Lord Jesus" is to destroy him "with the breath of his mouth." So, here in The Revelation, according to John, the triumph of the beast and his confederate kings is but "for one hour." Then we read, "These shall war against the Lamb, and the Lamb shall overcome them, for he is Lord of lords, and King of kings; and they also shall overcome that are with him, called and chosen and faithful." This is the important part of the vision. Whatever powers of evil may be denoted by Babylon and the beast, these enemies are to be overthrown. Christ is to reign as "King of kings," and his "called and chosen and faithful" followers are to share his glory.

By Babylon and the beast evidently John intended to picture the final forms of false religion and of political tyranny. He saw these prefigured and foreshadowed by the city and the empire of Rome. He looked for their perfect appearance at the end of the age, and immediately before the return of Christ. And this return seemed near. The age was already drawing to its close. In the language of John, it was "the last hour."

That hour has lengthened into centuries. The complete fulfillment of his prophecy is still future. Yet a partial realization of his vision is seen wherever a false religion assumes political power and dominates the state, or where a corrupt religious system is overthrown by a godless government. In a certain sense every era has its Babylon and every age has its beast.

2. THE FALL OF BABYLON   Ch. 18

1 After these things I saw another angel coming down out of heaven, having great authority; and the earth was lightened with his glory. 2 And he cried with a mighty voice, saying, Fallen, fallen is Babylon the great, and is become a habitation of demons, and a hold of every unclean spirit, and a hold of every unclean and hateful bird. 3 For by the wine of the wrath of her fornication all the nations are fallen; and the kings of the earth committed fornication with her, and the merchants of the earth waxed rich by the power of her wantonness.

4 And I heard another voice from heaven, saying, Come forth, my people, out of her, that ye have no fellowship with her sins, and that ye receive not of her plagues: 5 for her sins have reached even unto heaven, and God hath remembered her iniquities. 6 Render unto her even as she rendered, and double unto her the double according to her works: in the cup which she mingled, mingle unto her double. 7 How much soever she glorified herself, and waxed wanton, so much give her of torment and mourning: for she saith in her heart, I sit a queen, and am no widow, and shall in no wise see mourning. 8 Therefore in one day shall her plagues come, death, and mourning, and famine; and she shall be utterly burned with fire; for strong is the Lord God who judged her. 9 And the kings of the earth,

*who committed fornication and lived wantonly with her,
shall weep and wail over her, when they look upon the
smoke of her burning, 10 standing afar off for the fear of
her torment, saying, Woe, woe, the great city, Babylon, the
strong city! for in one hour is thy judgment come. 11 And
the merchants of the earth weep and mourn over her, for
no man buyeth their merchandise any more; 12 merchandise of gold, and silver, and precious stone, and pearls, and
fine linen, and purple, and silk, and scarlet; and all thyine
wood, and every vessel of ivory, and every vessel made of
most precious wood, and of brass, and iron, and marble;
13 and cinnamon, and spice, and incense, and ointment,
and frankincense, and wine, and oil, and fine flour, and
wheat, and cattle, and sheep; and* merchandise *of horses
and chariots and slaves; and souls of men. 14 And the
fruits which thy soul lusted after are gone from thee, and
all things that were dainty and sumptuous are perished from
thee, and* men *shall find them no more at all. 15 The merchants of these things, who were made rich by her, shall
stand afar off for the fear of her torment, weeping and
mourning; 16 saying, Woe, woe, the great city, she that
was arrayed in fine linen and purple and scarlet, and decked
with gold and precious stone and pearl! 17 for in one
hour so great riches is made desolate. And every ship-
master, and every one that saileth any whither, and mariners, and as many as gain their living by sea, stood afar
off, 18 and cried out as they looked upon the smoke of her
burning, saying, What city is like the great city? 19 And
they cast dust on their heads, and cried, weeping and
mourning, saying, Woe, woe, the great city, wherein all
that had their ships in the sea were made rich by reason
of her costliness! for in one hour is she made desolate.
20 Rejoice over her, thou heaven, and ye saints, and ye
apostles, and ye prophets; for God hath judged your judgment on her.*

*21 And a strong angel took up a stone as it were a great
millstone and cast it into the sea, saying, Thus with a
mighty fall shall Babylon, the great city, be cast down, and
shall be found no more at all. 22 And the voice of harpers
and minstrels and flute-players and trumpeters shall be
heard no more at all in thee; and no craftsman, of whatso-*

ever craft, shall be found any more at all in thee; and the
voice of a mill shall be heard no more at all in thee;   23
and the light of a lamp shall shine no more at all in thee;
and the voice of the bridegroom and of the bride shall be
heard no more at all in thee: for thy merchants were the
princes of the earth; for with thy sorcery were all the na-
tions deceived.   24 And in her was found the blood of
prophets and of saints, and of all that have been slain upon
the earth.

The literature of the world contains few passages which
compare in dramatic power with the scene of the fall of
Babylon as presented by the apostle John.   The scene is
not given in the form of a historic narrative or a prophetic
description, but voices are heard expressing thanksgiving
or dismay at the fate of the proud and profligate city.

The first voice is that of an angel "coming down out of
heaven."   So resplendent is his appearance that the earth
is "lightened with his glory."   He repeats and makes more
specific the sentence of doom already pronounced in
ch. 14:8: "Fallen, fallen is Babylon the great, and is become a habitation of demons, and a hold of every unclean
spirit, and a hold of every unclean and hateful bird."

The picture of coming desolation is heightened by the
intimation that the populous and active metropolis will
become, in its ruin, the haunt of wild and foul beasts.   So,
too, the overthrow of ancient Babylon was described by
Isaiah (Isa., ch. 13).

The angel then defines the guilt of the city, that the
justice of her fate may appear.   She has corrupted the nations; the kings have shared her impurities; the merchants
have been enriched by her luxuries; and now all are to
partake of her doom, "for by the wine of the wrath of her
fornication all the nations are fallen."

Suddenly a second voice is heard from heaven.   It
speaks for God himself.   It is a summons to the people of
God to leave the guilty city, that they may not share her
guilt and her ruin: "Come forth, my people, out of her,

that ye have no fellowship with her sins, and that ye receive not of her plagues."

This very call to escape deepens the impression of a doom that is imminent. Punishment is certain, "for her sins have reached even unto heaven, and God hath remembered her iniquities."

Therefore the command is addressed to the agents of divine justice, whoever these may be: "Render unto her even as she rendered, and double unto her the double according to her works: in the cup which she mingled, mingle unto her double." This does not mean that Babylon is to receive twice as much punishment as she deserves, as some have supposed, but that the measure of her sin must be the measure of her punishment. The essence of the sin is found in her pride and her luxury. These will be the occasion of sudden and complete ruin, for God is the Judge by whom sentence has been pronounced: "How much soever she glorified herself, and waxed wanton, so much give her of torment and mourning: for she saith in her heart, I sit a queen, and am no widow, and shall in no wise see mourning. Therefore in one day shall her plagues come, death, and mourning, and famine; and she shall be utterly burned with fire; for strong is the Lord God who judged her."

The actual scene of destruction is now presented in a series of lamentations chanted over the doomed city by the kings (Rev. 18:9-10), the merchants (vs. 11-17a), and the shipmasters (vs. 17b-19). The imagery is borrowed, as usual, from the Old Testament, particularly, in this case, from the prophecy of the destruction of Tyre. (Ezek., chs. 26; 27.)

The lament is begun by "the kings of the earth." They have shared in the impurity, the cruelty, and the selfish luxury of the great city. They stand afar off, fearing that they may share the pitiless doom, uttering their futile dirge: "Woe, woe, the great city, Babylon, the strong city! for in one hour is thy judgment come."

"The merchants of the earth" next are heard to "weep and mourn." Their sorrow is purely selfish. They are distressed that their chief mart is destroyed. Their merchandise will be left on their hands. This merchandise is listed with a vividness and detail possible only if the account was written by one who had seen something of the vast imports which flowed from the markets of the world toward imperial Rome. For the loss of their great patron, the merchants mourn in language which appears specially appropriate to them when compared with the lament of the kings: "Woe, woe, the great city, she that was arrayed in fine linen and purple and scarlet, and decked with gold and precious stone and pearl! for in one hour so great riches is made desolate."

A third lamentation is heard. It arises from the shipmasters and mariners, and from all who "gain their living by sea." Their interests are gravely affected by the fall of the city to whose unrivaled luxury they had ministered and by which they had secured their support. They "stood afar off, and cried out as they looked upon the smoke of her burning, saying, What city is like the great city? And they cast dust on their heads, and cried, weeping and mourning, saying, Woe, woe, the great city, wherein all that had their ships in the sea were made rich by reason of her costliness! for in one hour is she made desolate."

In contrast with these expressions of poignant grief, coming from kings and merchants and mariners, the voice from heaven calls upon saints, apostles, and prophets to rejoice in the destruction of their cruel enemy: "For God hath judged your judgment on her."

The voice from heaven has spoken. (Rev. 18:4-20.) In the solemn silence which follows, an angel appears and depicts the sudden and complete destruction of the city by a symbolic act: "A strong angel took up a stone as it were a great millstone and cast it into the sea, saying, Thus with a mighty fall shall Babylon, the great city, be cast down, and shall be found no more at all."

As a consequence of the disaster which is pictured by this dramatic action, all the pursuits that have made up the life of the city are brought to a tragic end. In contrast with her former festivity, and her busy craftsmen, her domestic labors and joys, all is silence and desolation and ruin. "The voice of harpers and minstrels and flute-players and trumpeters shall be heard no more at all in thee; and no craftsman, of whatsoever craft, shall be found any more at all in thee; and the voice of a mill shall be heard no more at all in thee; and the light of a lamp shall shine no more at all in thee; and the voice of the bride-groom and of the bride shall be heard no more at all in thee."

Why such destruction? Why is such a doom predicted? Because of the monstrous guilt of the sinful, cruel city. She has corrupted the kings and nations of the world. Her streets run red with the blood of Christian martyrs: "For thy merchants were the princes of the earth; for with thy sorcery were all the nations deceived. And in her was found the blood of prophets and of saints, and of all that have been slain upon the earth."

Such is the fall of Babylon; but what is Babylon? Not the ancient capital on the Euphrates, not the material city on the Tiber, but Rome as a spiritual symbol, Rome as reproducing the cruelty and power and luxury of Nebu-chadnezzar, Rome as the embodiment of all that is pagan and apostate and opposed to Christ. The picture has been realized in part by imperial Rome, and by papal Rome, and by godless cities and antichristian movements and systems. Just what the Babylon of the future may be none can predict. However, Babylon is not the apostate church of Christ. Babylon stands in hideous contrast to the church. One is the profligate "woman" who never has been true to God; the other is the pure bride of Christ. Babylon is the typical and relentless enemy of the church; and the fall of Babylon is depicted to encourage believers to endure all the suffering and persecution and martyrdom

that Babylon may inflict with the assurance that Christ
is certain to triumph over all his foes.

3. EPISODE: THE FOUR HALLELUJAHS
Ch. 19:1-10

*1 After these things I heard as it were a great voice of
a great multitude in heaven, saying,*

> *Hallelujah; Salvation, and glory, and power, belong
> to our God: 2 for true and righteous are his judg-
> ments; for he hath judged the great harlot, her that
> corrupted the earth with her fornication, and he hath
> avenged the blood of his servants at her hand.*

*3 And a second time they say, Hallelujah. And her smoke
goeth up for ever and ever. 4 And the four and twenty
elders and the four living creatures fell down and worshipped God that sitteth on the throne, saying, Amen;
Hallelujah. 5 And a voice came forth from the throne,
saying,*

> *Give praise to our God, all ye his servants, ye that
> fear him, the small and the great.*

*6 And I heard as it were the voice of a great multitude,
and as the voice of many waters, and as the voice of mighty
thunders, saying,*

> *Hallelujah: for the Lord our God, the Almighty,
> reigneth. 7 Let us rejoice and be exceeding glad,
> and let us give the glory unto him: for the marriage
> of the Lamb is come, and his wife hath made herself
> ready. 8 And it was given unto her that she should
> array herself in fine linen, bright* and *pure: for the
> fine linen is the righteous acts of the saints.*

*9 And he saith unto me, Write, Blessed are they that are
bidden to the marriage supper of the Lamb. And he saith
unto me, These are true words of God. 10 And I fell
down before his feet to worship him. And he saith unto
me, See thou do it not: I am a fellow-servant with thee and
with thy brethren that hold the testimony of Jesus: worship
God: for the testimony of Jesus is the spirit of prophecy.*

Between the fall of Babylon (ch. 18) and the fall of the
beast (ch. 19:11-21) an episode is introduced.   These

episodes are familiar features in all the great central sections of the book. As in the case of the other similar interludes, the thought here is turned both backward to the fall of Babylon and forward to "the marriage supper of the Lamb," which is to follow the destruction of his foes.

This interlude consists of a fourfold chorus. Each chorus embodies the same theme: "Hallelujah"—"Praise ye the Lord." The music of heaven has been heard often through the course of the prophecy, but not until now has been sounded the "Hallelujah Chorus." Nowhere else has the word "hallelujah" been employed. Indeed, nowhere else can it be found in the whole New Testament.

The first two hallelujahs celebrate the destruction of the profligate city, Babylon. The "voice of a great multitude in heaven" is heard, saying,

> "Hallelujah; Salvation, and glory, and power, belong to our God: for true and righteous are his judgments; for he hath judged the great harlot."

"And a second time they say, Hallelujah. And her smoke goeth up for ever and ever."

Real difficulty has been found in ascribing to heaven such a tragic and solemn song. Can saints rejoice in the doom of a great city or in the destruction of their foes? Is such music inspired by the Spirit of Christ? Let us not be hasty in our reply. We must distinguish between the sinner and the sin, between offenders and the offense. God who loves sinners hates sin. This is a moral universe. It would be impossible to believe that vice and virtue have the same reward, and that crime and cruelty and hate reach the same goal as innocence and sympathy and love. "The wages of sin is death." It cannot be otherwise. Heaven rejoices, not in the sufferings of men, but in the destruction of evil. Those who identify themselves with the life of Babylon must inevitably share her fate.

The larger and more important part of this interlude is an announcement of the marriage supper of the Lamb. In

this grand oratorio all the choirs of heaven unite. First
of all, "the four and twenty elders and the four living creatures fell down and worshipped God that sitteth on the
throne, saying, Amen; Hallelujah." Then "a voice came
forth from the throne," saying,

> "Give praise to our God, all ye his servants, ye that
> fear him, the small and the great."

Then the majestic chorus is heard, a chorus like "the voice
of a great multitude," like "the voice of many waters," like
"the voice of mighty thunders," saying:

> "Hallelujah: for the Lord our God, the Almighty,
> reigneth. Let us rejoice and be exceeding glad, and let
> us give the glory unto him: for the marriage of the Lamb
> is come, and his wife hath made herself ready. And it
> was given unto her that she should array herself in fine
> linen, bright and pure: for the fine linen is the righteous
> acts of the saints."

As the majestic chorus reaches its end, John hears a
voice commanding him to record what is the fourth of the
seven beatitudes found in The Revelation: "Write, Blessed
are they that are bidden to the marriage supper of the
Lamb." In solemn confirmation the claim is added,
"These are true words of God."

Completely overwhelmed by such a revelation from a
messenger of God, John "fell down before his feet to worship him." He is reassured, however, and is reminded of
the exalted character of his own prophetic task: "And he
saith unto me, See thou do it not; I am a fellow-servant
with thee and with thy brethren that hold the testimony of
Jesus: worship God." The special explanation is added
in a sentence of deep significance: "For the testimony of
Jesus is the spirit of prophecy." The question has been
raised whether the meaning here is "testimony borne by
Jesus" or "testimony borne to Jesus." Either would give
a true message. Probably the latter should be chosen

here. Witness to Jesus, as the Son of God, the Messiah, the Savior; witness to Jesus as the Lamb that was slain and as the coming King—this witness is "the spirit of prophecy"; it is the sum and substance, the inspiring theme, of all prophecy, whether of the Old Testament or the New, and all who are given the privilege of bearing witness to Jesus are fellow servants, members of one brotherhood.

What, then, is meant by "the marriage supper of the Lamb," the coming of which is announced with such exuberant joy? Evidently it is that perfect union with Christ, that final and complete blessedness of the church, which is more fully described in the closing chapters of the book (chs. 21; 22). The figure of marriage is a familiar one as used by the ancient prophets to express the relation of God to his people. The same figure was used frequently by Christ and his apostles in expressing the relationship between the heavenly Bridegroom and the church, his chosen bride. Thus, for example, Paul writes in his Epistle to the Ephesians, "Husbands, love your wives, even as Christ also loved the church, and gave himself up for it; that he might sanctify it, having cleansed it by the washing of water with the word, that he might present the church to himself a glorious church, not having spot or wrinkle or any such thing; but that it should be holy and without blemish."

Thus John and Paul both emphasize purity, holiness, and righteousness as the requisite preparation of the bride while she awaits the coming of the bridegroom and the joys of the marriage feast. Here John does not describe this marriage supper; he announces it, and declares its blessedness. First, the enemies of Christ must be destroyed. Then, in the dawning splendor of the golden age, the church will appear "as a bride adorned for her husband" (ch. 21:2). In view of the glorious city of God, an angel is heard, saying, "Come hither, I will show thee the bride, the wife of the Lamb" (v. 9).

4. THE FINAL JUDGMENTS   Chs. 19:11 to 20:15

a. The Beast and His Followers   Ch. 19:11-21

11 And I saw the heaven opened; and behold, a white horse, and he that sat thereon called Faithful and True; and in righteousness he doth judge and make war. 12 And his eyes are *a flame of fire, and upon his head* are *many diadems; and he hath a name written which no one knoweth but he himself. 13 And he is arrayed in a garment sprinkled with blood: and his name is called The Word of God. 14 And the armies which are in heaven followed him upon white horses, clothed in fine linen, white* and *pure. 15 And out of his mouth proceedeth a sharp sword, that with it he should smite the nations: and he shall rule them with a rod of iron: and he treadeth the winepress of the fierceness of the wrath of God, the Almighty. 16 And he hath on his garment and on his thigh a name written, KING OF KINGS, AND LORD OF LORDS.*

17 And I saw an angel standing in the sun; and he cried with a loud voice, saying to all the birds that fly in mid heaven, Come and *be gathered together unto the great supper of God; 18 that ye may eat the flesh of kings, and the flesh of captains, and the flesh of mighty men, and the flesh of horses and of them that sit thereon, and the flesh of all men, both free and bond, and small and great.*

19 And I saw the beast, and the kings of the earth, and their armies, gathered together to make war against him that sat upon the horse, and against his army. 20 And the beast was taken, and with him the false prophet that wrought the signs in his sight, wherewith he deceived them that had received the mark of the beast and them that worshipped his image: they two were cast alive into the lake of fire that burneth with brimstone: 21 and the rest were killed with the sword of him that sat upon the horse, even the sword *which came forth out of his mouth: and all the birds were filled with their flesh.*

Christ will return. The crucified and risen Savior will reappear. His coming is the hope of the world. He will bring peace between nation and nation, between heaven and earth, between God and man. The exact time or manner of his return has not been revealed; however, his coming has been the central message of The Revelation. Again and again in this prophecy the whole stage of history seems to have been set for his appearing. Usually a pause has occurred. The prophet has stopped to emphasize more fully some preparatory event. He has heightened the expectation of his readers. He has made them impatient of delay. Once, indeed, he has pictured the Son of Man seated on a cloud and reaping the harvest of the earth (ch. 14:14-16); but now, as the prophecy draws to its close, he describes in more striking symbols the coming of Christ, the destruction of his enemies (chs. 19:11 to 20:15), and the final blessedness of the church (chs. 21:1 to 22:5).

In this vision of the prophet the heaven is opened. Seated on "a white horse" is One who is called "Faithful and True." "His eyes are a flame of fire, and upon his head are many diadems. . . . He is arrayed in a garment sprinkled with blood: and his name is called The Word of God." The armies of heaven follow him. "Out of his mouth proceedeth a sharp sword." And "he treadeth the winepress of the fierceness of the wrath of God. . . . And he hath on his garment and on his thigh a name written, KING OF KINGS, AND LORD OF LORDS." Against him are gathered "the beast, and the kings of the earth, and their armies"; but the beast is taken, and "with him the false prophet," and "they two" are "cast alive into the lake of fire." Their followers are killed "with the sword of him that sat upon the horse," and all the birds of prey are "filled with their flesh."

All this is symbolism at its highest. No one imagines that such statements are literal. Never shall we see the "white horse," the sword projecting from the mouth of the conqueror, or the birds gorged with the flesh of fallen warriors. However, this is not mere feverish fancy. There are facts which correspond to these figures. The symbols are intended to express vital realities. They must be interpreted with caution and humility. Yet something of their meaning must be manifest to all who read.

First of all, and in the light of other prophetic Scriptures, it is evident that the return of Christ is to be the glorious climax of all human history. When and how and where this return will be manifested, no one can affirm. Yet it is to be an event by which his triumph is to be consummated and his rule is to become perfect and universal. Undoubtedly there is now a blessed reality in his spiritual presence; beyond question he moves through the unfolding eras of history; but, in contrast with his unseen presence, there is to be a visible appearing. At the goal of all historical process there is to be a crisis. There is one event toward which the whole creation is moving. From this one event will date the perfected Kingdom of God upon earth. This event is the personal, visible return of Christ.

In the second place, it appears, with less definiteness of prediction, that his followers will be delivered from the judgments which are to fall upon his foes and will share in his victory. The armies which follow him from heaven, "clothed in fine linen, white and pure," include not only angels, but glorified saints. Out of great tribulation, having been "caught up . . . to meet the Lord in the air," with their robes washed in the blood of the Lamb, they swell the triumph of his train. Just what such predictions may include, one can only conjecture. Enough is clear to give confidence to all who are true to their Lord. They first must endure persecution and suffering for his sake. They ever must keep themselves pure, that when he shall appear they may have confidence and "not be ashamed before him at his coming." But they are certain to share his triumph and glory.

Most emphatic of all is the message which forms the uniform background in each vision of The Revelation. It is the message that evil surely will be overthrown. Here it is presented in a picture of almost repellent realism. When the armies of earth go forth to meet the armies of heaven, no battle is described. Only an angel voice is heard, "saying to all the birds that fly in mid heaven, Come and be gathered together unto the great supper of God; that ye may eat the flesh of kings, and the flesh of captains, and the flesh of mighty men, and the flesh of horses and of them that sit thereon, and the flesh of all men, both free and bond, and small and great."

The figure seems to have been borrowed from the prophet Ezekiel. (Ezek. 39:17-20.) However, it appears to be also a solemn travesty upon the marriage supper of the Lamb, the announcement of which introduced this scene of punishment. All those who belong to Christ are invited to the feast, at which they will enjoy perfect union and fellowship with him. All the followers of the beast will be found at "the great supper of God," where their flesh will be consumed by foul birds of prey.

Thus comes the assurance that by the final judgments of God every form and embodiment of political tyranny and of false religion will be destroyed. In the figurative language of John, the beast and the false prophet will be "cast alive into the lake of fire." For their followers, and for all who are allied with them, judgment is no less certain. They will afford an unholy banquet for the agents of divine wrath and will be devoured at the dreadful supper of God.

b. The Dragon   Ch. 20:1-10

1 And I saw an angel coming down out of heaven, having the key of the abyss and a great chain in his hand. 2 And he laid hold on the dragon, the old serpent, which is the Devil and Satan, and bound him for a thousand years, 3 and cast him into the abyss, and shut it, and sealed it over him, that he should deceive the nations no more, until the thousand years should be finished: after this he must be loosed for a little time.

4 And I saw thrones, and they sat upon them, and judgment was given unto them: and I saw the souls of them that had been beheaded for the testimony of Jesus, and for the word of God, and such as worshipped not the beast, neither his image, and received not the mark upon their forehead and upon their hand; and they lived, and reigned with Christ a thousand years. 5 The rest of the dead lived not until the thousand years should be finished. This is the first resurrection. 6 Blessed and holy is he that hath part in the first resurrection: over these the second death hath no power; but they shall be priests of God and of Christ, and shall reign with him a thousand years.

7 And when the thousand years are finished, Satan shall be loosed out of his prison, 8 and shall come forth to deceive the nations which are in the four corners of the earth, Gog and Magog, to gather them together to the war: the number of whom is as the sand of the sea. 9 And they went up over the breadth of the earth, and compassed the camp of the saints about, and the beloved city: and fire came down out of heaven, and devoured them. 10 And the devil that deceived them was cast into the lake of fire and brimstone, where are also the beast and the false prophet; and they shall be tormented day and night for ever and ever.

After the destruction of the beast and the false prophet, the interest next is centered upon the destruction of the dragon. The great truth symbolized is clear and vital. It is this: it is not enough to overthrow the agents or instruments of evil, but evil itself must be overthrown. It is not enough to cast the beast and the false prophet into the lake of fire; the devil, who has empowered them, must share their doom. War cannot be ended by pacifism or militarism, not by treatise or by leagues, while hate and malice and lust for power rule the hearts of men. A better social order cannot be secured by political revolution but only by the reign of love. Thus the judgment of Satan must precede the perfected Kingdom of God.

This destruction of the dragon is pictured in two stages.

First, he is bound and cast into "the abyss." Then, after "a thousand years," he is "loosed for a little time." He gathers the nations against "the camp of the saints," but is overwhelmed and is consigned to endless torment.

This cryptic and mysterious section must be interpreted with diffidence and with generous appreciation of the many devout students who hold differing views. It may not be unfair to intimate that some interpreters are misled by centering their thoughts upon the "thousand years," the millennium, rather than upon the imprisonment of Satan, of which the thousand years are the measure, and upon his final overthrow, when the thousand years are ended. Whatever the millennium may mean, its mention is rather incidental to the doom of the dragon, with which this vision is concerned.

Do the events depicted by this vision follow, or are they parallel to those of the vision which precedes (ch. 9:11-21)? Is there to be a second gathering of the armies of the world against Christ and his church, or do we have here a further description of the same event, given to emphasize the final destruction of the very power and principle of evil by which the enemies of Christ have been inspired? Probably this is the determining question in every endeavor to discover the meaning of this disputed passage.

Those who hold the former view accept the following as a general outline of the events which are predicted: The return of Christ results in the defeat of the beast and his followers; then Satan is bound and the world enjoys a millennium of peace and blessedness; the risen saints rule with Christ; Jerusalem is the seat of power; then Satan is "loosed," and gathers the nations "as the sand of the sea" against the Holy City; fire from heaven devours the nations which have come from "the four corners of the earth"; Satan is cast into the lake of fire; then follows the final judgment, and, at last, "a new heaven and a new earth."

Such seems to be the sequence of events if the two visions follow each other in the order of time. However, this view should be held with caution and reserve. It is beset by many difficulties. One of the chief is the fact that no such millennium is mentioned in any other part of the Bible. It will be found that, when carefully examined, the passages which are supposed to be parallel refer to a reign of Christ which is endless, to a Kingdom of God which is perfected "for ever and ever." No limited period of ten centuries of peace, with a tragic ending in universal war, can be discovered on any other page of inspired prophecy.

Then again, the events which other passages of Scripture associate with the return of Christ seem to allow no extended period of time between that climactic event and their occurrence. At the coming of Christ the dead will be raised, "all the nations" will appear before the throne of his glory, all enemies will be destroyed, and his endless reign will begin. Such appears to be the predicted order. It is rather difficult to establish the familiar view of two bodily resurrections separated by a period of a thousand years, or of a judgment of "all the nations" (Matt. 25:32), at the beginning of the millennium, and of a second universal judgment, before the "great white throne," at the end of the millennium (Rev. 20:11-15). It is also open to question whether or not the prophet intends to describe two battles, one thousand years apart, each apparently a final conflict between Christ and his foes. The former battle is said to include "the kings of the earth, and their armies" and "all men, both free and bond." These are destroyed. Can there then be a second and different conflict, in which are engaged other "nations," "the number of whom is as the sand of the sea," which cover "the four corners" and "the breadth of the earth" (vs. 8-9)?

The more serious objection to this view, however, is not to its general outline, but to the additions which many of its advocates attach to this framework of events. Even those who accept such an outline feel that it is precarious to insist upon certain of the following items which the theory commonly includes: (1) a coming of Christ for his saints before the career of "the man of sin" and the "great tribulation," and another coming of Christ with his saints, seven years later, to destroy "the man of sin"; (2) a "first resurrection" of all believers and a "rapture of the church," before "the man of sin" appears, and then another resurrection of believers, here described by John as "the first resurrection," in which those have a part who have been martyrs under "the man of sin"; (3) such changes in nature, before the time of the new heaven and the new earth, that the Old Testament prophecies will be fulfilled literally: "The lion shall eat straw like the ox" wild beasts "will become meek and tame"; the life of man will be lengthened, so that "a man of one hundred years will be esteemed but a child"; (4) Israel will be converted, but will form a body distinct from the Christian church; (5) Jerusalem will be enlarged and adorned and be the capital of the Jewish people, who will rule "the nations of the world"; (6) the Temple will be rebuilt and animal sacrifices reestablished; (7) Christians of all past ages will appear upon earth in glorified bodies, and, with Christ and with Israel, will reign over all the world, until Satan is again set free to involve in a universal war those nations which for a thousand years have known the blessings of the glorious reign of Christ.

Some of these items seem to contain contradictions or to be fanciful and at variance with the teachings of Scripture. Consequently, many students prefer to follow, in its main features, the interpretation accepted by Augustine and other expositors, ancient and modern. They attempt to evade the difficulties of the preceding theory by regarding the vision of the destruction of Satan (ch. 20:7-10) as parallel to the preceding vision of the destruction of the beast and the false prophet (ch. 19:19-21).

According to this view, the binding of Satan was accomplished by the incarnation and the atoning work of

Christ. The final overthrow of Satan will be accomplished by the triumphant return of Christ. The "thousand years" measures the present age, the period between the defeat of Satan and his ultimate doom.

Such a theory is obviously absurd, if the "thousand years" is a phrase intended to denote an age of universal righteousness and peace. It is tragically true that such a millennium does not now exist. But did John intend to designate the future age of glory by the term "a thousand years"? It may seem futile to attempt now to interpret the word "millennium" in any other sense. However, much can be said in support of this theory, which holds that the age of glory will not come until Satan, as well as his forces and followers, has been destroyed, and that the golden age, the real era of righteousness and peace, the perfected Kingdom of God, is described, not in the terms of a limited thousand years (ch. 20), but in the inspired picture of a new heaven and a new earth (chs. 21; 22).

However, if the "thousand years" is supposed to have begun with the binding of Satan accomplished by Christ at his first advent it appears fair to object that this binding of Satan is pitifully inadequate and incomplete. Yet it must be admitted that our Lord and his apostles use even stronger words than "binding" and "imprisonment" to describe the effect upon Satan produced by Christ's redeeming work. Christ not only claims that he has bound Satan, "the strong man" whose "house" he has entered; but he declares, as he stands under the shadow of the cross: "The prince of this world hath been judged"; "Now shall the prince of this world be cast out." And the apostle affirms that Christ became incarnate and suffered on the cross, in order "that through death he might bring to nought him that had the power of death, that is, the devil." Thus, in the view of Scripture, Satan is a defeated foe. Already he has been seen to fall from heaven (Luke 10:18); already he has been "bound" (Matt. 12:22-29). At least in principle he has been "cast out" and even "destroyed," but undoubtedly his restricted power is actually continuing; his agents still are mighty and malignant. At the end of the age, as all agree, he will summon the nations to a final attack upon the people of God, "the camp of the saints." Then, as predicted by the prophet, his doom will be sealed; fire will come "down out of heaven" to devour his followers, and the devil will be "cast into the lake of fire and brimstone."

Despite its evident difficulties, it must be admitted that this theory is in accordance with the literary structure of The Revelation. The visions of John are not to be understood as indicating a sequence in time. They are largely repetitious and parallel. The same scene is thrown upon the screen a second or a third time, that all the light of prophetic revelation may be focused upon a single event.

Thus it is quite possible that John does not have in mind two distinct universal conflicts, one at the end of a subsequent "millennial age." Indeed, all those battles which he describes, each of which seems to be caused by a final outbreak of unprecedented evil, may be one. The innumerable horsemen of the sixth trumpet (Rev. 9:16), and the gathering of "the kings of the whole world" at Har-Magedon, of the sixth bowl (ch. 16:14, 16), and "the kings of the earth, and their armies," destroyed with the beast in the last preceding vision (ch. 19:19) may be the same as this great gathering of all the nations, "Gog and Magog," when the dragon is pictured as making his last assault upon the forces of God and as meeting his final doom (ch. 20:7-10).

This theory likewise conforms to the symbolic character of the book. It regards the entire paragraph as highly and wholly figurative. It is free from all misleading literalism and materialism. It does not suppose that the writer is attempting to describe the character of a future age, but is depicting the doom of Satan. As to the age of glory, it regards this as the theme of the two chapters which follow (chs. 21; 22). It considers that this vision is representing the conquest of evil and the overthrow of the dragon, which must be complete before the world can rejoice in the light of the City of God. It holds that, in language entirely symbolic, here is depicted the crushing defeat of Satan which Christ administered at his first advent, and that ultimate and absolute overthrow to be accomplished when Christ comes again.

It is important to notice further that this theory, whatever its weakness, accords well with the practical purpose of the book. Every vision is determined by one controlling aim. It is designed to encourage believers patiently to endure suffering and even martyrdom for the cause of Christ. Here the encouragement is given not only, as was just emphasized, by the assurance that Satan is already a defeated foe, but by the further assurance that to die for the sake of Christ is to enter at once into the heavenly glory of Christ, to "suffer with him" is to "reign with him." Thus the parenthetic picture of the saints, living and enthroned, while not the chief feature of the vision, is regarded as an essential and significant part. (Ch. 20:4-6.)

Between the picture of the binding of Satan and that of his final overthrow, just after the statement that "he must be loosed for a little time," occurs this comforting scene of the saints in glory. It indicates that, no matter what Satan may do, even in the time of his final and fiercest outburst of wrath, the people of God are secure. Some will be safe on earth, although besieged by innumerable foes; others will be reigning with Christ in heaven, even though they have passed thither by the cruel path of martyrdom.

Thus the prophet declares, "I saw thrones, and they sat upon them, and judgment was given unto them: and I saw the souls of them that had been beheaded for the testimony of Jesus, and for the word of God, and such as worshipped not the beast, . . . and they lived, and reigned with Christ a thousand years." Thus both those who suffer as martyrs and all who are true to Christ during the present age depart, in the hour of death, to "be with Christ," which "is very far better."

In earlier sections of The Revelation, John has carried out this same purpose of comfort in the same way. In the hours of greatest darkness and tribulation he has assured the followers of Christ that they need not fear. When the sixth seal was opened and heaven and earth were filled with portents and disaster, he beheld "a great multitude, which no man could number, . . . standing before the throne and before the Lamb, arrayed in white robes, and palms in their hands." They had "come out of the great tribulation, and they washed their robes, and made them white in the blood of the Lamb." (Ch. 7:9-17.)

When the beast and the false prophet were in full career, when the great tribulation was at its height, John saw "the Lamb standing on the mount Zion, and with him a hundred and forty and four thousand, having his name, and the name of his Father, written on their foreheads," and he heard them singing a new song, while "harpers" were "harping with their harps." (Ch. 14:1-5.)

So here, it is argued, as the dragon is about to manifest his fiercest and final outburst of wrath, there comes this heartening vision of the glory shared by the saints and martyrs who have gone to be with Christ. Their experience is termed "the first resurrection." It is not the spiritual resurrection by which New Testament writers describe the entrance upon a Christian life, nor is it the bodily resurrection which takes place at the coming of Christ. It is a figurative and symbolic description of the experience of all who, by the gateway of death, enter into the presence of Christ. "Blessed and holy is he that hath part in the first resurrection," writes the apostle: "over these the second death hath no power." They have suffered death once, but they are in no danger of that "second death," which is designated also "the lake of fire."

"They shall be priests of God and of Christ, and shall reign with him a thousand years."

This theory which makes the "thousand years" a symbol of the present age, and regards the age of gold as the period described by "a new heaven and a new earth," is quite in accord with the New Testament description of the present era. The theory does involve the serious paradox of a dragon who is "bound" and "cast out" and "destroyed," yet a dragon in actual exercise of his power and about to be "loosed," that he may lead to final conflict and defeat all the nations of the world. Both phases of truth must be kept in view. Satan is a defeated foe. Christ has "bound" and "destroyed" him—this in principle and by the power of the cross. However, Satan is still active and is awaiting eagerly the hour of his most violent attack upon the people of God.

Such a view guards the church against the superficial optimism which expects the present age to develop gradually into the perfected Kingdom of God without further persecution and independently of the glorious appearing and intervention of Christ. It guards against an equally mistaken pessimism, which views the world as now going from bad to worse until the condition is so desperate that Christ must return.

The Scriptures, rather, seem to teach that the present age is one of mingled good and evil. The gospel is being preached, the cause of Christ is being advanced, and the devil is unable to stay the progress and development and beneficent activities of the church. However, the followers of Christ must expect no present exemption from struggle, no freedom from opposition, no release from persecution. Through much tribulation the Kingdom of God will come. Still, there is no ground for discouragement and despair. The fiercest onslaught of the enemy will result only in his utter defeat and final doom.

To the theory considered thus at length, weighty objections will be raised. The same probably is true of other proposed solutions of the problem. None of the attempts at interpreting this vision (ch. 20:1-10) appears to be free from difficulties. None should be presented with dogmatic assurance. It is quite possible, as many students suppose, that before the ultimate triumph of Christ there may intervene a preliminary age fulfilling the popular dream of a millennium. Or it may be that the return of our Lord will introduce an age in which the farthest vision can discern no shadow of coming disaster, no horizon bounded by a "thousand years." Whatever view may be held, it must be helpful to remember that this perplexing passage is not concerned chiefly with the description of an era of holiness and peace but with a prediction of the overthrow of Satan. By a few bold strokes the author depicts first the restraint and then the final defeat of that archenemy of Christ, who must be destroyed before the vision can be realized of the City of God descending to earth from heaven.

c. The Dead   Ch. 20:11-15

11 And I saw a great white throne, and him that sat upon it, from whose face the earth and the heaven fled away; and there was found no place for them. 12 And I saw the dead, the great and the small, standing before the throne; and books were opened: and another book was opened, which is the book of life: and the dead were judged out of the things which were writen in the books, according to their works. 13 And the sea gave up the dead that were in it; and death and Hades gave up the dead that were in them: and they were judged every man according to their works. 14 And death and Hades were cast into the lake of fire. This is the second death, even the lake of fire. 15 And if any was not found written in the book of life, he was cast into the lake of fire.

The doctrine of future punishments and rewards forms an essential element in the system of Christian faith. The fact that these are described in symbolic language should make the punishments seem no less dread and the rewards no less glorious. Both are beyond the power of human speech to express.

As in the prophecies of the Old Testament, judgments upon guilty nations are predicted as preceding the perfected Kingdom of the Messiah, so in The Revelation a series of judgments is related as introducing the age of glory which is designated by the term "a new heaven and a new earth." These judgments include the doom of Babylon and of the beast, the destruction of the dragon, and finally the judgment of the dead.

Apparently the prophet here has in view the impenitent dead. No doubt, the righteous are likewise to be judged, "for we must all be made manifest before the judgment-seat of Christ." However, in this vision the thought seems to be centered upon the fate of the wicked. The purpose is to show that, on the return of Christ, not only the beast and the dragon and their living followers are to be overthrown, but all their subjects and confederates, who previously have passed into the realm of death, are to partake of the same doom. The intention is to describe the complete condemnation and overthrow of evil before painting the picture of the age of gold.

The writer uses no lurid colors in setting forth the Last Judgment. He manifests becoming restraint and reserve. He does not describe the scene in detail, nor does he locate it in space or time. He declares that he "saw a great white throne." It is "great," as denoting the power of the Judge who sits upon the throne. It is "white," as indicating the absolute justice which there is dispensed. From the face of this Judge "the earth and the heaven fled away," a figure of speech which denotes that heaven and earth are not worthy to stand before the infinite holiness of God.

"The dead, the great and the small," were seen "standing before the throne." It is implied that a resurrection had taken place. This resurrection is described in the following verse. At least, it is stated that "the sea gave up the dead that were in it; and death and Hades gave up the dead that were in them." To the prophet on his sea-girt isle, the "great deep" was a symbol and a scene of death. Furthermore, he indicates that all who were in their graves were likewise to rise, all who had passed under the power of death and had experienced the condition of the dead were to stand before the throne.

"They were judged every man according to their works." This is the main point of the message. Judgment is to be universal, and it is to be just. Each one will receive "according to what" he has "done in the body, . . . whether it be good or bad."

The judgment will be in accordance with clear evidence: "Books were opened: . . . and the dead were judged out of the things which were written in the books, according to their works." The figure of written books denotes a record and a remembrance of all the deeds of each one who stands for judgment before the "great white throne."

Another book is mentioned. It is "the book of life." Apparently this is the roll of those who are citizens of the New Jerusalem. Nothing is here specified as to their fate. Undoubtedly they are to enter upon eternal glory. It is stated, however, that "if any was not found written in the book of life, he was cast into the lake of fire." Such a statement cannot fail to strike the reader with awe. Nothing could be more solemn than this scene. Yet its purpose must be kept in mind. It is not intended to record merely the punishment of the impenitent, but to set forth the final defeat of all the enemies of Christ and his church. "Death and Hades" also are "cast into the lake of fire." Both death and all its consequences are forever destroyed. The triumph of Christ is complete.

G. THE NEW JERUSALEM   Chs. 21:1 to 22:5

1. INTRODUCTORY VISION: THE NEW HEAVEN AND THE NEW EARTH   Ch. 21:1-8

1 And I saw a new heaven and a new earth: for the first heaven and the first earth are passed away; and the sea is no more. 2 And I saw the holy city, new Jerusalem, coming down out of heaven from God, made ready as a bride adorned for her husband. 3 And I heard a great voice out of the throne saying, Behold, the tabernacle of God is with men, and he shall dwell with them, and they shall be his peoples, and God himself shall be with them, and be their God: 4 and he shall wipe away every tear from their eyes; and death shall be no more; neither shall there be mourning, nor crying, nor pain, any more: the first things are passed away. 5 And he that sitteth on the throne said, Behold, I make all things new. And he saith, Write: for these words are faithful and true. 6 And he said unto me, They are come to pass. I am the Alpha and the Omega, the beginning and the end. I will give unto him that is athirst of the fountain of the water of life freely. 7 He that overcometh shall inherit these things; and I will be his God, and he shall be my son. 8 But for the fearful, and unbelieving, and abominable, and murderers, and fornicators, and sorcerers, and idolaters, and all liars, their part shall be in the lake that burneth with fire and brimstone; which is the second death.

This earth is yet to see its age of glory and of gold. Pagan poets and philosophers commonly pictured such an age as belonging to the past; but in the sacred Scriptures inspired prophets predict this era as one which the future holds in store. John designates it by the phrase, "A new heaven and a new earth." This phrase is taken from Isa. 65:17; 66:22. By it the ancient seer did not describe a new solar system and a new planet, but indicated a great moral and spiritual revolution by which the people of God would be delivered from their imperfections and distress, brought back from their exile, and given undoubted prosperity and peace and joy in the land of their fathers and in the city of their sacred memories and blessed hopes.

So when the apostle Peter adds to the figure more lurid colors, to paint the scene of the return of Christ and of the events which will introduce the age of glory (II Peter 3:7), he declares that we are looking for "new heavens and a new earth, wherein dwelleth righteousness" (v. 13); and he compares the dissolving of the world to the Flood, which did not destroy the globe but did introduce a better age.

Thus when John here speaks of "a new heaven and a new earth" he is not intimating that a new physical universe of stars and a new world are to be created, but he is declaring that an age is to dawn, so much better and more glorious than this present age that it well may be described, in the words of Isaiah, as "a new heaven and a new earth." It is that age to which Christ referred when he spoke of "the regeneration when the Son of man shall sit on the throne of his glory" (Matt. 19:28). Peter refers to this age when he urges his hearers to repent: "That so there may come seasons of refreshing from the presence of the Lord; and that he may send the Christ who hath been appointed for you, even Jesus: whom the heaven must receive until the times of restoration of all things, whereof God spake by the mouth of his holy prophets that have been from of old" (Acts 3:19-21).

This renewed "earth," this rejuvenated world, this age of endless peace, John describes first negatively, by a striking symbol: "The sea is no more" (Rev. 21:1).

Evidently, therefore, he does not refer to a prior destruction of this earth, for then of course the mountains and cities and forests, as well as the sea, would no longer exist. He is using a figure of speech to express an era in which evil and distress no longer exist. Many of us love the sea. We know that it is necessary to the very life of

the world. The Hebrews, however, were a pastoral people. They stood in dread of the great sea. John was a
prisoner on a small, bleak, rocky, seagirt island. It can
easily be imagined what the sea may have meant to him.
It was the symbol of mystery, of separation, of restless-
ness, of futility, of danger, and of death. The world will
indeed be blessed, he thinks, when "the sea is no more."

The positive side of that blessedness is pictured by the
figure of "the holy city, new Jerusalem, coming down out
of heaven from God, made ready as a bride adorned for
her husband." This "city," as John explains (v. 9), is
the church of Christ. It is the focal point of all the glory
of the age to come. A description of that city occupies
the closing vision of the Apocalypse. (Chs. 21:9 to 22:5.)
The absence of "the sea" and the presence of this "city"
form a large factor of this preparatory vision. (Ch.
21:1-8.)

There is, however, another even more important and
closely related factor. It is the presence of God, and fellowship with him, which forms the essential feature of the
age to come: "I heard a great voice out of the throne
saying, Behold, the tabernacle of God is with men,
and he shall dwell with them, and they shall be his peoples, and God himself shall be with them, and be their
God."

The picture is taken from the encampment of Israel in
the wilderness. Around the tabernacle, "the dwelling
place of Jehovah," the twelve tribes were grouped in
orderly array. So, in the age to come, the nations of the
world will rejoice in the manifested presence of God in
their midst.

The result will be more marvelous than words can express. It can at least be suggested by stating the conse-
quent banishment of all that shadows and saddens the
age in which we live: "God . . . shall wipe away every
tear from their eyes; and death shall be no more; neither
shall there be mourning, nor crying, nor pain, any more."

All these former or "first things" shall have "passed away."

As to the fulfillment of this radiant hope there need be no doubt. Divine assurance has been given: "He that sitteth on the throne said, Behold, I make all things new. And he saith, Write: for these words are faithful and true. And he said unto me, They are come to pass. I am the Alpha and the Omega, the beginning and the end."

Who are to share this infinite felicity of the age to come? All who so desire, all who are willing to pay the price, all who triumph over persecution and temptation and sin, all who are true to Christ: "I will give unto him that is athirst of the fountain of the water of life freely. He that overcometh shall inherit these things; and I will be his God, and he shall be my son."

Grave choices are being made in this present age. Every man decides the way his soul shall go: "For the fearful, and unbelieving, and abominable, and murderers, and fornicators, and sorcerers, and idolators, and all liars, their part shall be in the lake that burneth with fire and brimstone; which is the second death."

With these latter solemn words John points his readers back to the scene which precedes (ch. 20:11-15), just as by this general description of the new heaven and the new earth he prepares them for the vision which is now to follow, the vision of the City of God (chs. 21:9 to 22:5).

2. THE GLORY AND BLESSEDNESS OF THE HOLY CITY   Chs. 21:9 to 22:5

9 And there came one of the seven angels who had the seven bowls, who were laden with the seven last plagues; and he spake with me, saying, Come hither, I will show thee the bride, the wife of the Lamb. 10 And he carried me away in the Spirit to a mountain great and high, and showed me the holy city Jerusalem, coming down out of heaven from God, 11 having the glory of God: her light was like unto a stone most precious, as it were a jasper stone, clear as crystal: *12 having a wall great and high; having twelve gates, and at the gates twelve angels; and names written thereon, which are* the names *of the twelve tribes of the children of Israel: 13 on the east were three gates; and on the north three gates; and on the south three gates; and on the west three gates. 14 And the wall of the city had twelve foundations, and on them twelve names of the twelve apostles of the Lamb. 15 And he that spake with me had for a measure a golden reed to measure the city, and the gates thereof, and the wall thereof. 16 And the city lieth foursquare, and the length thereof is as great as the breadth: and he measured the city with the reed, twelve thousand furlongs: the length and the breadth and the height thereof are equal. 17 And he measured the wall thereof, a hundred and forty and four cubits,* according to *the measure of a man, that is, of an angel. 18 And the building of the wall thereof was jasper: and the city was pure gold, like unto pure glass. 19 The foundations of the wall of the city were adorned with all manner of precious stones. The first foundation was jasper; the second, sapphire; the third, chalcedony; the fourth, emerald; 20 the fifth, sardonyx; the sixth, sardius; the seventh, chrysolite; the eighth, beryl; the ninth, topaz; the tenth, chrysoprase; the eleventh, jacinth; the twelfth, amethyst. 21 And the twelve gates were twelve pearls; each one of the several gates was of one pearl: and the street of the city was pure gold, as it were transparent glass. 22 And I saw no temple therein: for the Lord God the Almighty, and the Lamb, are the temple thereof. 23 And the city hath no need of the sun, neither of the moon, to shine upon it: for the glory of God did lighten it, and the lamp thereof is the Lamb. 24 And the nations shall walk amidst the light thereof: and the kings of the earth bring their glory into it. 25 And the gates thereof shall in no wise be shut by day (for there shall be no night there): 26 and they shall bring the glory and the honor of the nations into it: 27 and there shall in no wise enter into it anything unclean, or he that maketh an abomination and a lie: but only they that are written in the Lamb's book of life. 22:1 And he showed me a river of water of life, bright as crystal, proceeding out of the throne of God and of the Lamb, 2 in the midst of the street thereof. And on this side of the river and on that was the tree of life, bearing twelve manner of fruits, yielding its fruit every month: and the leaves of the tree were for the healing of the nations. 3 And there shall be no curse any more: and the throne of God and of the Lamb shall be therein: and his servants shall serve him; 4 and they shall see his face; and his name shall be on their foreheads. 5 And there shall be night no more; and they need no light of lamp, neither light of sun; for the Lord God shall give them light: and they shall reign for ever and ever.*

"Jerusalem the golden" means heaven. At least, it does to most people and in common speech. It is well that it does, for the picture of the Holy City painted by John has been the solace and inspiration of countless saints and sufferers through all the ages. It has been the expression of their highest hopes, the symbol of all their future joys. As descriptive of life in some distant celestial sphere, it has been the substance of sermons, of poems, and of rapturous songs. Surely such hopes will not deceive. "To be absent from the body, and to be at home with the Lord," will be an experience no less blessed, but far more glorious, than residence in such a city as John is supposed to describe.

In reality, however, John is not picturing a scene in some distant heaven. He is recording a vision of the church of Christ on earth. He is concerned, not with a place, but with a people. He is employing physical objects to represent spiritual realities. The church he describes is an ideal church. It now exists, but its perfected splendor will appear in the age to come. This City, already founded and now being built, will form the central glory of the new heaven and the new earth.

This "beloved city" was mentioned previously, surrounded by the hosts of Satan, as the "thousand years" were coming to their disastrous end. (Ch. 20:7-9.) In the vision of the "new earth," the "holy city" was seen "coming down out of heaven from God" (ch. 21:2). In this vision which follows, John is given a nearer and more perfect view of "the holy city Jerusalem." He declares the city to be, not a distant abode of the saints, but to be the church, "the bride, the wife of the Lamb."

The angel to whom John owes the vision (vs. 9-10) may have been the same that invited him to behold the doom of Babylon; and the two cities are thus brought into intentional contrast, the apostate city and the heavenly "bride." In further contrast with "the wilderness" in which the persecuted church was seen (ch. 12:6), John is now carried away "to a mountain great and high," whence he obtains a rapturous and clear vision of "the holy city Jerusalem, coming down out of heaven from God." He has caught previously a glimpse of this descending city. (Ch. 21:2.) Now he sees and describes the City in detail, dwelling first upon its structure and glory (vs. 9-27), and then upon its inner life and blessedness (ch. 22:1-5).

The first feature of this glory is its radiance: "Having the glory of God." The visible cloud, the "pillar of fire," the "shekinah" which rested upon and illumined the Holy of Holies in the ancient tabernacle, has its actual counterpart in the divine Presence which dwells within the church and shines in the hearts and lives of men. As a consequence of this indwelling Presence the "light," which the City sheds abroad, is "like unto a stone most precious, as it were a jasper stone, clear as crystal."

The wall of the City, "great and high," may picture its security, or its definite outline and its beauty. These walls have "twelve gates" or "gate towers" or "portals," through which access is gained. At each gate is an angel watcher or guardian, probably not to prohibit entrance but to make admission certain and joyous.

Three gates open toward each point of the compass, to indicate free and universal access to God and to fellowship with his people. On the gates are written "the names of the twelve tribes of the children of Israel," and on the "twelve foundations" of the walls the "names of the twelve apostles of the Lamb." Thus the saints of the Old Testament and of the New are all one, united in the blessedness of the Holy City. As has been observed, the four essential notes of the church appear in this vision: "unity, holiness, catholicity, and apostolicity."

To express the greatness of the City, the angel measures it with "a golden reed" and discovers that "the length and the breadth and the height thereof are equal," each dimension being "twelve thousand furlongs." To regard as literal such poetic imagery would result in a picture absurd and grotesque. The prophet surely does not conceive a material city fifteen hundred miles in length and breadth and height. By the symbol of a perfect cube, like the Holy of Holies in the tabernacle, he indicates the perfection of the church, and the holiness of the body of Christ.

The splendor of the City is further emphasized by mention of the materials of which it is built. "The wall thereof" is jasper, and in contrast the City itself gleams like a mass of gold, so "pure" that it seems to be as transparent as glass. "The foundations of the wall of the city" are "adorned with all manner of precious stones." These gems correspond in large measure to those on the breastplate of the high priest (Ex. 28:17-20). In John's vision each stone is of immeasurable size. "The twelve gates" are "twelve pearls." (Rev. 21:21.) "The street of the city"—thus even things of the most servile use—is "pure gold," so like "transparent glass" that one seems to look into and through it as he walks upon it.

"I saw no temple therein." None is needed. The entire City is a Holy of Holies. The universal presence of God makes it one spacious sanctuary: "For the Lord God the Almighty, and the Lamb, are the temple thereof." The symbol is not needed when the reality has come.

Then, also, as the City requires no material temple because of the abiding presence of God, so too it needs no created light: "The city hath no need of the sun, neither of the moon, to shine upon it: for the glory of God did lighten it, and the lamp thereof is the Lamb."

The City sheds its radiance upon the surrounding nations. Such is true of the church which now is "the light of the world," and such it will be in the ages to come, until all the earth is filled with the knowledge of God: "The nations shall walk amidst the light thereof."

Into this City shall be brought all that is precious, all that is great and good, for "the kings of the earth bring their glory into it." Even now it is possible for the representatives of all nations, turning to Christ, to make some addition to the strength and perfection of the church; and in the age to come, through the open gates of the City of Light, all the riches of the redeemed earth shall be brought into its treasure house. The gates are never shut. Nevertheless from that City all corruption and evil are excluded forever: "There shall in no wise enter into it anything unclean, or he that maketh an abomination and a lie: but only they that are written in the Lamb's book of life."

Such phrases prepare us for the final vision of the heavenly Jerusalem, by which our thought is turned from its radiant structure to the blessedness of its inner life. (Ch. 22:1-5.) As the Bible opens with the story of "Paradise Lost," so it here closes with a picture of "Paradise Regained." The first paradise was a garden, and here is a picture of a garden in a city. It is a city, because redeemed humanity will form a society, a community, a church. It is a garden, for all that Eden offered will be realized fully in the paradise to come.

"He showed me a river of water of life," that is, a river whose waters give life in all its fullness. It proceeds "out of the throne of God and of the Lamb," and it pours its crystal stream through the midst of the broad street of the City. Of such a river the psalmist sang—of one indeed whose streams shall "make glad the city of God." Are not these the streams of divine truth applied by the Spirit of God to refresh and strengthen the people of God?

As the Garden of Eden had its flowing river and its tree of life, so, in this new paradise, on both sides of the river stand the trees of life, "bearing twelve manner of fruits," yielding their fruit every month. Thus everything speaks of life, of life more abundant, of life continually supported and sustained. "And the leaves of the tree" are "for the healing of the nations"; for the church has been placed in the world to share with all people the life which faith in Christ secures. True blessedness consists, not in selfish enjoyment even of the life of paradise, but in providing for others spiritual healing and enrichment.

"And there shall be no curse any more." There was a curse pronounced in Eden. Sin issued in pain, in isolation, and in death. In the heavenly Jerusalem all the results of sin are done away. For the redeemed there is pardon and peace and immortal joy.

"And the throne of God and of the Lamb shall be therein." This is a picture of perfect rule, and of a government which is divine. The redeemed already know something of this blessed Kingdom; but the whole creation awaits its glorious consummation.

"And his servants shall serve him," with a service which is perfect freedom and unalloyed delight. Even now there is no service so joyous, so fruitful, so glad, as the service of God; but then the priestly ministry will be free from all weariness, all imperfection, all restraint.

"And they shall see his face." Even here "the pure in heart" can "see God." They behold his glory "in the face of Jesus Christ." Yet "now we see in a mirror, darkly"; then the beautiful vision will be unclouded and complete.

As a consequence his likeness will be stamped upon his servants: "His name shall be on their foreheads." "We shall be like him; for we shall see him even as he is."

"And there shall be night no more." This same feature of glory has been mentioned before. (Ch. 21:25.) There it indicated why the gates of the City never need be closed, and that access to God is always possible. Here it implies that the blessed service of the saints never need be interrupted. In each case the reason is the same. There is a divine Source of unfailing light: "The Lord God shall give them light."

"And they shall reign for ever and ever." The redeemed are indeed priests, but they all are kings. They share the royal rule of their Lord. The promise to them is for no limited "millennium," no "thousand years," but "for ever and ever."

Such is John's vision of the Holy City. Such is the ideal church. Some rays of its glory already can be seen. God grants us even now some understanding of "the riches of the glory of his inheritance in the saints." The glowing symbols of the prophet enable us to discern the faint outlines of the City of God, but the full manifestation of its glory awaits an age yet to dawn. It will appear only when the Kingdom for which we pray has been perfected. It can come only with the coming of the King.

III
THE EPILOGUE
Ch. 22:6-21

6 And he said unto me, These words are faithful and true: and the Lord, the God of the spirits of the prophets, sent his angel to show unto his servants the things which must shortly come to pass. 7 And behold, I come quickly. Blessed is he that keepeth the words of the prophecy of this book.

8 And I John am he that heard and saw these things. And when I heard and saw, I fell down to worship before the feet of the angel that showed me these things. 9 And he saith unto me, See thou do it not: I am a fellow-servant with thee and with thy brethren the prophets, and with them that keep the words of this book: worship God.

10 And he saith unto me, Seal not up the words of the prophecy of this book; for the time is at hand. 11 He that is unrighteous, let him do unrighteousness still: and he that is filthy, let him be made filthy still: and he that is righteous, let him do righteousness still: and he that is holy, let him be made holy still. 12 Behold, I come quickly; and my reward is with me, to render to each man according as his work is. 13 I am the Alpha and the Omega, the first and the last, the beginning and the end. 14 Blessed are they that wash their robes, that they may have the right to come to the tree of life, and may enter in by the gates into the city. 15 Without are the dogs, and the sorcerers, and the fornicators, and the murderers, and the idolaters, and every one that loveth and maketh a lie.

16 I Jesus have sent mine angel to testify unto you these things for the churches. I am the root and the offspring of David, the bright, the morning star.

17 And the Spirit and the bride say, Come. And he that heareth, let him say, Come. And he that is athirst, let him come: he that will, let him take the water of life freely.

18 I testify unto every man that heareth the words of the prophecy of this book, If any man shall add unto them,

God shall add unto him the plagues which are written in this book: 19 and if any man shall take away from the words of the book of this prophecy, God shall take away his part from the tree of life, and out of the holy city, which are written in this book.

20 He who testifieth these things saith, Yea: I come quickly. Amen: come, Lord Jesus.

21 The grace of the Lord Jesus be with the saints.

                                                        Amen.

The sentences of the last section in this unique prophecy are somewhat disconnected and abrupt. This is a natural, even an artistic, feature of an epilogue such as these sentences form. The great ideas of the entire book are repeated in the brief, striking statements, with no attempt at an exact sequence of thought. However, a real unity is given to this epilogue by the recurrence of two dominant notes—the notes of certainty and of imminence. The prophecies of the book are certain of fulfillment, and that fulfillment is near at hand. Thus, the very substance of this concluding section consists in the confirmation of the prophecy by the interpreting angel, by John, and by Christ, and in the reechoing promise of the Lord himself: "Behold, I come quickly."

The first voice is that of the angel: "These words are faithful and true." He refers to the words of the entire revelation. Speaking of himself in the third person, he adds, "The Lord, the God of the spirits of the prophets, sent his angel to show unto his servants the things which must shortly come to pass." Then the voice of Christ is heard, possibly speaking through the angel: "Behold, I come quickly." To this promise a beatitude is added: "Blessed is he that keepeth the words of the prophecy of this book." One is reminded of the prologue (ch. 1:1-8). The parallels are numerous and should be carefully noted. At least, here is the blessing again pronounced upon those who carefully read and faithfully observe and patiently obey the messages of this inspired prophecy.

In view of all the astonishing visions, and especially of

the climactic scene of the Holy City, it is not strange that John is overwhelmed with emotion, and that he falls at the feet of the angel in an attitude of worship. However, as in a previous experience, he is reminded by the angel that both are servants of God, to whom alone all adoration and reverence and praise are due: "He saith unto me, See thou do it not: I am a fellow-servant with thee and with thy brethren the prophets, and with them that keep the words of this book: worship God." It is probably true that all those today whose sight is illumined to see something of the spiritual splendors of The Revelation will not neglect it as an unsolved enigma, but will praise and adore Him who has given us in mysterious symbols glimpses of ineffable glory.

Because the coming of Christ is regarded as near, these words are added: "Seal not up the words of the prophecy of this book; for the time is at hand." The visions are not to be kept secret as though referring to a distant day. They belong to the present, and the end of the age is regarded as about to appear. To the mind of the prophet there is little time now for repentance and a change of life. The deliberate choice of each man has fixed his unalterable fate. Character will continue to produce its inevitable development and fruit: "He that is unrighteous, let him do unrighteousness still: and he that is filthy, let him be made filthy still: and he that is righteous, let him do righteousness still: and he that is holy, let him be made holy still."

There comes a time when the chosen course cannot be altered. There is a solemn reality in the words, "Too late." However, there is rapturous joy for those who have chosen Christ and have been true to him, when they hear his glad assurance: "Behold, I come quickly; and my reward is with me, to render to each man according as his work is."

Then is added the claim made by Christ of being one with the Father, for he employs the same terms as are found in the prologue as coming from "the Almighty": "I am the Alpha and the Omega, the first and the last, the beginning and the end." As "all things were made through him," so to him as their goal all things move. Thus, for those who have chosen him as Redeemer and Master and Lord, another beatitude is added: "Blessed are they that wash their robes, that they may have the right to come to the tree of life, and may enter in by the gates into the city."

Not all may enter. Choices are being made. Some are rejecting the Savior. Some must be excluded from the City of Light: "Without are the dogs," the symbol of all that is offensive, uncontrolled, unclean, "and the sorcerers, and the fornicators, and the murderers, and the idolaters, and every one that loveth and maketh a lie."

Christ now adds his further attestation to the book: "I Jesus have sent mine angel to testify unto you these things for the churches." He adds this precious word of description: "I am the root and the offspring of David," and as such he is the Fulfillment of all that was promised to the heir of David's throne; he is the predicted Messiah, "the King of Kings, and Lord of Lords."

He is "the bright, the morning star." This star shines most brightly just before the break of day. So the coming Christ is the Hope of all nations. His return will bring the dawning of an age of radiant light.

To this blessed assurance of his return the church makes answer, "The Spirit and the bride say, Come." "The Spirit," speaking through the prophets and the saints of all the ages, inspires this glad response. Then comes the exhortation, addressed to each individual who has heard the words of this prophecy, "And he that heareth, let him say, Come."

To this is added the gracious invitation to everyone who is longing for life in its fullness, for satisfaction and peace: "He that is athirst, let him come: he that will, let him take the water of life freely."

As a blessing was attached to the reading and the proper "keeping" of this book, so there is a solemn warning against its abuse: "I testify unto every man that heareth the words of the prophecy of this book, If any man shall add unto them, God shall add unto him the plagues which are written in this book: and if any man shall take away from the words of the book of this prophecy, God shall take away his part from the tree of life, and out of the holy city, which are written in this book."

This arresting warning must refer to any willful perversion and distortion of the great truths which The Revelation contains. One cannot fail, however, to find in it a certain implied caution to all who, however honestly, seek to set forth its meaning and to interpret its mysterious symbols. All dogmatism must be put aside, all unkind insinuations as to those who differ, and all self-confident assumption of infallibility and omniscience. Much of the book will probably never be understood fully until reviewed in the glory of the coming age. The book must not be neglected; but grave responsibility rests on all who undertake to teach its precious and inspiring truths. Even though sincere, those who allow the book to form a basis for unbridled fancy or a ground for bitter dispute and controversy cannot be excused from serious fault and blame. "We know in part, and we prophesy in part." However, we do know. It is beyond question that this book was written to encourage all believers to be patient in persecution, steadfast in days of trial and tribulation, assured that to be loyal to Christ is to be on the side of right, of truth, of ultimate triumph, and of eternal joy.

Finally, the book closes with a promise, a prayer, and a benediction. The living Christ who has confirmed the prophecy gives his word of hope and cheer, embodying the very essence of the inspired message: "He who testifieth these things saith, Yea: I come quickly." From every loving heart comes the prayerful response, "Amen: come, Lord Jesus."

John adds the unusual benediction, "The grace of the Lord Jesus be with the saints. Amen." Let us not suppose that this blessing rests on any special group of favored souls. All who believe in Christ and serve and love him are "saints." They are "holy," because purchased by his precious blood and separated unto his service and "joint-heirs" of his eternal glory. All can depend upon him for "grace" in every hour of need. All can overcome and enter at last into the City of Light. All should unite in the earnest and confident prayer, "Amen: come, Lord Jesus."